Creative Science Classrooms

by Sandra Markle

SCHOLASTIC
PROFESSIONAL BOOKS

New York • Toronto • London • Auckland • Sydney

For
Lucille Kimball, Edyphe Louys,
Nate Vance, Vera Eger,
Dorothy Link, and Doug Thompson,
special teachers
whose creativity made learning
meaningful, memorable, and fun
when I was growing up
in Fostoria, Ohio.

S.M.

For information regarding permission, write to
Scholastic Inc., 730 Broadway, New York, NY 10003.

Designed by Design 5
Cover design by Vincent Ceci
Cover photograph by Richard Hutchings
Illustrations by Loretta Lustig

ISBN 0-590-49072-9

Contents

The activities presented in Instructor Books' *Creative Science Classrooms* will have students personally discovering science facts and concepts by performing hands-on investigations. More important, these activities will provide children with opportunities to think creatively by applying science facts and concepts in problem-solving situations. And learning to tackle problem-solving situations creatively is essential to understanding science as it relates to today's increasingly technological world.

Consumer Science, Investigating Change, A Little Bit Wild, and Mini Field Trips— each exploratory unit has its own special focus. The extensive support materials will help you teach these concepts through hands-on discovery experiences that will excite students about science. Each unit begins with Getting Started, a step-by-step lesson guide that will have kids actively participating in a creative problem-solving activity and start them thinking about investigating the topic. Next, Bulletin Board Ideas will help you turn your display areas into interactive learning centers. And finally, Using the Activities will help you make each lesson an exciting learning experience.

Your guide to each individual unit lesson provides everything you need to start students thinking and to help them tackle the activity creatively. There is a list of supplies needed to perform the activity, and background information on the specific topic covered by the discovery experience. Teaching Strategies presents a step-by-step approach to introduce the lesson, teach the concept—often in several different ways, so you can tailor the material to your students' needs and classroom situation—and draw conclusions from the lesson by applying the concept. The Teaching Strategies are always developed with the four main stages of an effective hands-on science lesson in mind—the motivational starter, data collecting, data processing, and closure. Each lesson guide also includes Extenders, which will provide ideas for applying the concept or suggestions for ways to tie this highly motivational science learning experience to other subject areas. Answers to the activity sheets are included and a list of sources suggests juvenile books for students interested in exploring further.

The hands-on activities in *Creative Science Classrooms* are designed to encourage students to use the six basic science-process skills—observing, classifying, measuring, communicating, inferring, and predicting—as investigative tools. And each exploratory unit is developed in a way that encourages students to think creatively as they tackle problem-solving situations.

With the practice provided by *Creative Science Classrooms*, the science-process skills will become familiar investigative tools and creative thinking will become a natural approach to problem solving. After all, inquiry and knowing how to search for an answer are what science is all about.

Effective Class Management for Creative Science Classroom Activities

One of the easiest ways to ensure that your students will work in an organized way and stay on task is to divide your class into cooperative task groups. A cooperative task group is made up of no more than five or six students who work on the activity together, sharing duties in a specific, predetermined way. Each cooperative task group has a member responsible for one of the following jobs:

Principal Investigator: This person is in charge of the group. He or she is the only one to whom you've given specific instructions on how to perform the investigation. The P.I. keeps the group on task. And only the P.I. may come to you if the group has a question during the investigation.

Materials Manager: This person collects any materials the group needs. You may provide this person with a list of things to collect from a supply area. Or you may presort materials into boxes and have the materials manager simply pick up his or her group's box. If the group is large enough, a second Materials Manager can be assigned to be responsible for returning materials to the supply area and having the group clean up their work area.

Recorder: This person may need to keep a written record of the group's observations. If the activity includes a test, each person in the group will perform the test, and this person will record the results on a group chart or graph.

Reporter: This person writes down the group's conclusion and reports to the class. The reporter may also need to record the group's data on a class graph or chart.

This super-organized approach helps make hands-on discovery activities and problem-solving tasks flow smoothly and keeps the lid on unnecessary noise created by too many people moving around. It also encourages all students to take leadership roles as they take their turn at being principal investigator. You may want to make badges to help students identify with their role and to let you know who has what job.

Getting Started

Catch everyone's attention by playing a tape recording of a popular radio advertisement or a videotape of a television commercial. Discuss together how the commercial captured its audience and in what ways it made the product appealing. Next, assign a half hour of television viewing as homework and tell your students to pay special attention to the commercials. Have them make a list of which products they see advertised and describe the ad they like best. Allow time for students to share what they discover. Compile a class list of what features your students believe make a "good" commercial, meaning one that makes the product seem appealing and memorable.

Have your students conduct a survey of other classes and their family members to identify the three currently playing television commercials people like best. Point out that by saying they like the commercial people are showing that the commercial has succeeded in making the product appealing and memorable. If possible, tape the winning three to view together as a class. Challenge your students to analyze these commercials, deciding what makes them winners. After completing the activities for this unit, view these commercials again and decide which of the basic advertising techniques they use (see Decoding Ads, p. 7) and how they capture the viewer's attention.

Bulletin Board Ideas

1. For Sale: Collect print advertisements that clearly use one of the seven basic advertising techniques (testimonial, bandwagon, positive appeal, negative appeal, product character, slogan, and comparison). Mount these on sheets of colored construction paper and number each one. Then make one pocket (by stapling together three sides of large sheets of colored construction paper or using large manila envelopes with the tops cut off) for each category and write the name of that category on the front of the pocket. At the top of the bulletin board, place directions to decide which advertising technique is used in each ad and place that ad in the correct pocket. To make this a self-checking activity, tape an answer flap on the outside of the pocket. Under this flap, list the numbers of the advertisement that used that particular technique.

2. Personal Appeal: It's possible to sell people as well as products. Perhaps the most obvious example of this is a presidential election. Challenge your students to consider themselves a candidate for president even if it's a nonelection year. Then have each child design his or her own campaign poster using one of the advertising techniques presented in Decoding Ads (p. 7). If it's an election year, also have students bring in actual campaign posters and ads for display. Decide together which advertising technique is being used in each ad.

Decoding Ads......................

Directions: Analyze each of the seven basic advertising techniques described below. Then decide which technique is being used to push each of the pretend products.

Testimonial: Someone famous tells you the product is wonderful.

Bandwagon: The ads says everybody's buying this product so you should, too.

Positive Appeal: The ad makes you think that having this product will make you happier or more appealing to other people.

Negative Appeal: The ad makes you afraid that not having this product could make you unhappy, uncomfortable, or even sick.

Product Character: An appealing live or cartoon character represents the product.

Slogan: You can't forget this catchy phrase.

Comparison: Compared with other brands, this is the best choice.

1. Your hair can be beautiful, too, if you use Shiny Shampoo. I wouldn't use anything else. _____

2. Don't be the last kid in your class to put your feet in Super Sneaks.

_____

3. Brighto outcleans all the leading brands.

_____

4. A message from the Washington Apple Twins: 'Only the biggest, juiciest apples go into Squishy Applesauce.'

_____

Product Pushers...................

Directions: Watch television for one hour. Pay special attention to the commercials as you complete the chart below.

Product Advertised	Advertising Technique (Testimonial, Bandwagon, Positive Appeal, Negative Appeal, Product Character, Slogan Comparison)
_____	_____
_____	_____
_____	_____
_____	_____
_____	_____
_____	_____
_____	_____
_____	_____
_____	_____
_____	_____

1. Advertisers count on repetition to help you remember their products. List any products you saw advertised more than once. _____

_____

2. Of all the commercials you've seen recently, which one did you like best? _____

_____

3. What advertising technique did it use?_____

_____

• Use the back of this page if you need more room.

..........Product Pushers..........

Buyer's Choice..........................

Directions: List the brand your family chooses most often for each of the items listed below. Check one or more of the reasons your family selects this particular brand. You may need to discuss these choices with your family.

Brand	Purchased because of its		
	Special Features	**Price**	**Advertising Claims**
Bread: _____			
Peanut butter: _____			
Margarine: _____			
Orange juice: _____			
Breakfast cereal: _____			
Soft drink: _____			
Shampoo: _____			
Laundry detergent: _____			

BONUS CHALLENGE ★★★★★★★

What kind of advertising influences your family most—print, radio, or television? Discuss this with your family.

_____

_____

_____

_____

A Sure Sign..........................

Advertisers use symbols to help customers quickly identify specific brand-name products.

Directions: List your favorite brand. Then cut out and paste the symbol (or draw and color a picture of the symbol) for that brand next to its name.

Fast food   _____

Soft drink   _____

Jeans   _____

Tennis shoes   _____

Automobile   _____

Toothpaste   _____

Fresh Approach ....

Directions: Decide what advertising technique is being used to promote Purr-fect cat food in the ad below. Then choose a different technique and create your own advertisement for this product.

"Cat lovers everywhere buy Purr-fect cat food for their pets."

1. What advertising technique does this ad use? _____

2. What advertising technique will you use? _____

Purr-fect cat food (Your advertisement)

Checking Out the Claims...
1: The Paper Race

Which brand of paper towel absorbs water fastest?

Directions: Answer the questions as you perform the test to find out. You'll need one sheet of at least four different brands of paper towels, a ruler, scissors, a quart jar, red food coloring, a pencil, tape, a permanent marker, and a clock with a second hand.

1. Examine the paper towels closely. How do the towels differ?

_____

_____

2. Which brand of paper towel do you think will absorb water fastest? Why?

_____

_____

Now follow the steps below to test your prediction.

- Cut three strips 2 inches wide and 10 inches long from each paper towel. Keep these strips in separate piles. List the brand names of the towels on the chart.

- Next, partly fill the quart jar with water and add several drops of red food coloring. Then tape one end of one of the paper towel strips to the pencil.

- Touch just the edge of the free end of the towel to the water's surface and hold it there for 10 seconds.

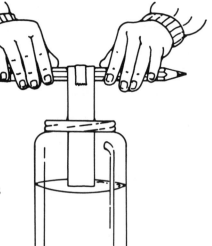

Checking Out the Claims ....
1: The Paper Race (continued)

- The water will move through the paper towel. As soon as the time is up, make a dot with the marker to show how far up the paper towel the water traveled and take the towel out of the jar. It's important to mark the water level immediately because the water will continue to rise in the towel even after the strip is removed from the water. Record the results on the chart.

- Repeat this test with each of the other strips. Add more water to the jar as needed.

Paper Towels	Test 1	Test 2	Test 3	Average Distance

- Figure the average distance the water rose. (To compute the average, add the results of all three tests. Then divide that total by three.)

3. Which paper towel absorbed water fastest?_____

4. Examine the winning paper towel again. Why do you think this paper towel was able to absorb water so quickly?_____

_____

_____

_____

Checking Out the Claims ...
2: That Tears It

Which paper towel is strongest when wet?

Directions: Answer the questions as you perform this test to find out. You'll need one sheet of at least four different brands of paper towels, tape, two pencils, two identical quart jars, a measuring cup, a small terry-cloth towel, and pennies.

1. Examine the paper towels closely. How do the towels differ?

_____

_____

_____

_____

2. Which brand of paper towel do you think will be strongest when wet? Why?

_____

_____

_____

_____

Now follow the steps below to test your prediction.

• Tape one end of a paper towel to the side of one pencil. Tape the other end to the other pencil. Place one pencil across the mouth of each quart jar and spread the jars apart until the paper is stretched tight.

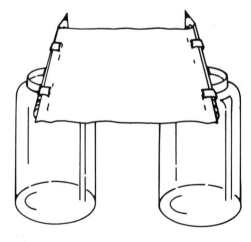

Checking Out the Claims ....
2: That Tears It (continued)

- Place the terry-cloth towel carefully under the paper. Then pour one-quarter cup of water slowly onto the center of the paper towel.

- After the water stops dripping through, have someone hold on to each pencil and jar to anchor them in place. Begin placing pennies on the wet part of the paper towel one at a time until the paper tears, dropping its load. Record the results on the chart.

- Repeat this test with each of the other paper towels.

Paper Towels	Test 1	Test 2	Test 3	Average

- Figure the average number of pennies. (To compute the average, add up the results of all three tests. Then divide that total by three.)

3. Which paper towel was strongest when wet? _____

4. Examine the winning paper towel again. Why do you think this paper towel was able to hold more pennies while wet than the others?_____

_____

Checking Out the Claims ...
3: Suds and More Suds

Which liquid dishwashing soap produces the most suds?

Directions: Answer the questions as you perform the test to find out. You'll need four self-sealing plastic sandwich bags, four identical clear plastic cups, a marking pen, four different brands of liquid dishwashing soap, measuring spoons, a measuring cup, warm water, a ruler, and a clock with a second hand.

1. Use your sight, smell*, and sense of touch to examine the four different liquid

dishwashing soaps. How are the soaps alike? _____

_____

2. How are the soaps different? _____

_____

3. Predict which soap will produce the most suds._____

On what did you base your prediction? (Was it an advertising claim or something

about the soap itself?)_____

_____

Record the names of the soaps on the chart. Pour one-quarter cup of warm water into a plastic bag. Add one-quarter teaspoon of one of the liquid dishwashing soaps. Seal the bag and shake vigorously for 10 seconds. Quickly mark the bottom and top of the suds layer. Measure the distance between these two lines. Record this information on the chart. Then repeat this test with each of the other types of soap.

Kind of Soap　　　　　　　**Inches of Suds**

_____

_____

_____

_____

* Remember to sniff safely. Hold the soap about 6 inches from your nose and wave your hand above it, fanning the air toward your nose.

Name:_____

Checking Out the Claims...
4: Come Clean

Does one brand of detergent really do a better job of removing food stains than another?

Directions: Answer the questions as you perform this test to find out. You'll need four identical 2-inch squares of plain cotton cloth, ketchup, warm water, a permanent marker, four different laundry detergents, four self-sealing plastic sandwich bags, a measuring cup, and measuring spoons.

1. Use your sight, smell*, and sense of touch to examine the four different laundry

detergents. How are they alike? _____

_____

_____

2. How are the laundry detergents different? _____

_____

_____

3. Predict which detergent will do the best job of cleaning stains._____

On what did you base this prediction? (Was it an advertising claim or something

about the detergent itself?_____

_____

_____

_____

Turn page for more...

* Remember to sniff safely. Hold the soap about 6 inches from your nose and wave your hand above it, fanning the air toward your nose.

Checking Out the Claims ....
4: Come Clean (continued)

: **Now write the names of the four detergents on the chart and follow the steps below**
: **to test how well each one cleans.**

• Smear one-half teaspoon of ketchup on each cloth square and let the stains dry. Then draw around the stains with the marker.

• Pour one-half cup of warm water and one teaspoon of one of the laundry detergents into each plastic bag. Put a strip of paper tape on each bag and write the name of the detergent that was added on the tape.

• Put one cloth square into each bag, seal, and shake vigorously for 15 seconds. Pour off the water. Add another half-cup of clean water, seal and shake five seconds more. Squeeze out the cloth and let the squares dry. Compare the outlined areas.

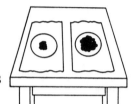

Types of Detergent	Stain Removal - Judge on a scale of 1 (dirtiest) to 10 (cleanest)
_____	
_____	
_____	

4. Why was it important to make the amount of water, type of stain, amount of detergent, and length of time shaken identical for each detergent tested?

_____

_____

5. State a fact about the laundry detergent that did the best cleaning job.

_____

_____

6. State an opinion about this detergent. _____

_____

_____

Fact or Opinion?.....................

Can you tell the difference when advertisers make claims about their products?

Directions: Read each of the advertising claims listed below. Put an F next to each statement that lists a fact and an O next to each opinion. Remember, only statistics and the results of scientific research provide facts about a product. Words like *best*, *preferred*, and *favorite* reveal that what's being presented is really someone's opinion.

1. The best detergent is Super White. _____

2. Ten out of twelve laundry experts preferred Super White. _____

3. Super White contains 0.03% phosphate. _____

4. Super White contains more phosphate than Dirt Buster. _____

5. Super White is the President's favorite detergent. _____

6. Housewives surveyed said they loved Super White. _____

7. Super White contains bleach for extra whiteness. _____

8. Sales of Super White increased last year by 25%. _____

Name: _____

Thirst Quencher...................

Is there a difference between fruit juice and fruit drink?

Directions: Complete the product survey below and then draw your own conclusion.

1. Fill in the chart below, listing three brands of fruit juice and three products that are labeled fruit drinks.

2. Next, read each product's label. Record the percentage of real juice each contains and how much sugar, if any, is added.

Fruit Juices	% Real Juice	Sugar Added
A. _____		
B. _____		
C. _____		
Drinks D. _____		
E. _____		
F. _____		

3. Which of the products that you investigated do you think is best for you?
_____ Why? _____
_____
_____

4. What's the main difference you discovered between fruit juices and fruit drinks?
_____
_____
_____

Name: _____

Hot Dog?..................................

What are you eating when you chomp on a hot dog?

Directions: Answer the questions as you perform the investigation below. Remember, manufacturers are required to list a product's ingredients, and the first three items on the list show the main ingredients used in preparing that product.

1. Visit a grocery store and read the label on at least four different brands of hot dogs (or wieners). How many brands did you check? _____

How many listed meat as one of the first three ingredients? _____

2. Which meat was most commonly listed as an ingredient in hot dogs?

_____

3. Other than meat, what else was among the top three ingredients?

_____

_____

4. Perform a cooking test on at least two brands to find out how much the hot dogs shrink during cooking. First, record the brand names and precooking information on the chart below. Next, cook each hot dog by boiling it in a pan of water for two minutes. wear an oven mitt and use tongs to carefully remove the hot dog from the water, or have an adult partner do this for you. After the hot dog has cooled, remeasure it.

Hot Dog	Length		Weight	
	Before	**After**	**Before**	**After**

Smart Shopper......................

Directions: Pretend that you have $20 to spend. You can buy any nonfood item you want. Go shopping and list what you think you'd like to buy. Then answer the questions to decide if this product would be a smart choice.

I want to buy _____.

1. Does it appear well made?   Yes ☐   No ☐

2. Do you know anyone who has been pleased with the product?   Yes ☐   No ☐

3. Do you think it's really worth what it costs?   Yes ☐   No ☐

4. Is it something that's likely to be cheaper later?   Yes ☐   No ☐

5. Does it compare well with similar products that cost less?   Yes ☐   No ☐

6. It is something you're likely to be able to enjoy for a long time?   Yes ☐   No ☐

7. Now, look over your checklist. Do you think this product would

be a smart purchase?   Yes ☐   No ☐

8. Why? _____

_____

Using the Activities

Decoding Ads
(p. 7)
Product Pushers
(p. 8)
Buyer's Choice
(p. 9)
A Sure Sign
(p. 10)
Fresh Approach
(p. 11)

Supplies

A copy of each of the worksheets for each child.

Background Information

Advertisements are something designed to call attention to a product, and ads are everywhere. They may be simple or elaborate. Sometimes television ads are even more entertaining than the programs they interrupt. It's important, however, to understand that the purpose of advertising is to sell. To do that job, advertisers use seven basic techniques.

In the testimonial, someone famous or at least popular tells about the product's features. They generally imply that they personally use and recommend that product. With personal care products particularly there is also the implication that by using that product, the consumer will somehow be more like the person presenting the ad.

The bandwagon technique makes every effort to express the idea that absolutely everyone else is now using the product so, of course, you should, too.

The *positive* appeal and *negative* appeal advertisements have the same basic goal—to show that being happy and successful requires using a specific product. In the positive appeal, consumers are made to believe that using a product will make them happy, more appealing, or whatever. In the negative appeal, consumers are made to think that without the product they'll be unhappy, unappealing, or whatever.

The *comparison* technique is designed to eliminate the competition. These advertisements name other brands—often more popular ones—and explain how those products are inferior.

The product character approach and the slogan are both designed to make a specific brand the one that leaps to mind when you're ready to buy. Most people, for example, would recognize a certain hamburger-pushing clown on sight and could sing at least one soft drink commercial.

Understanding how advertisements are designed to make products appealing can help consumers get beyond ad appeal when evaluating a product's real worth.

Teaching Strategies

Use the Decoding Ads activity to introduce students to the seven basic advertising techniques. Discuss the seven techniques, allow a few minutes for students to perform the activity, then go over the responses. Replay the commercial you used to introduce this unit and decide together which technique was used to make this product appealing.

Have students perform Product Pushers, Buyer' Choice, and A Sure Sign as take-home activities. Display the completed copies of the A Sure Sign activity for everyone to see the symbols. Allow time to discuss the results of Product Pushers and compile the data from the Buyer's Choice family survey to find out which brands are most popular. Then discuss whether this is a result of some special features, price, or successful advertising.

Finally, challenge your students to apply what they discovered by having them work in small groups to tackle the problem-solving situation provided in the Fresh Approach activity. Allow time for the groups to present their new advertisement. Have the other groups identify the advertising techniques used in these new, original ads.

Extenders

1. New Twist: Videotape a popular commercial for a familiar product. Play this for your class and analyze it. Discuss which technique is used to push the product.

Have students work in small groups to prepare a new commercial for this product. Assign each group to take a different approach based on one of the advertising techniques not used by the commercial. Keep these assignments secret. Allow time for the groups to present their commercials. If possible, videotape the commercials to play back. Challenge the class to identify the new techniques the groups used. Vote on which approach provides the most effective product push.

2. Buy and Buy: Compile a class list of commercials students feel are aimed at them. Discuss together what techniques product pushers are using to make them want to buy. Come to a class conclusion about ways students could defend themselves from making purchases based on commercials rather than product analysis.

Answers

Decoding Ads: 1. Testimonial; 2. Bandwagon; 3. Comparison; 4. Product Character. **Product Pushers:** Chart and 1–3. Answers

23

will vary but should reflect logical response to commercials viewed. **Buyer's Choice:** Answers will vary but should provide obviously real data based on products listed; Bonus Challenge: Answers will vary. **A Sure Sign:** Answers will vary. **Fresh Approach:** 1. Bandwagon; 2. Answers will vary; Advertisements will vary but should be creative and done in style listed in No. 2.

Resources

Be a Smart Shopper by Kathlyn Gay. Englewood Cliffs, New Jersey, Julian Messner, 1974.
The Food Peddlers by Martha C. Mapes and Patricia Thonney. New York State College of Human Ecology and the New York State College of Agriculture and Life Sciences, Cornell University, Ithaca, New York, 1985.
The School on Madison Avenue: Advertising and What It Teaches by Ann E. Weiss. New York: E.P. Dutton, 1980.

Checking Out the Claims
1: The Paper Race
(pp. 12–13)
2: That Tears It
(pp. 14–15)
3: Suds and More Suds
(p. 16)
4: Come Clean
(pp. 17–18)

Supplies

A copy of each of the worksheets for each child.

Background Information

To test whether a product can really perform as advertised, it's important to follow good scientific methods. Three kinds of variable (something that can change) will be involved in every test—the

manipulated variable, the responding variable, and the controlled variable. The manipulated variable is the thing being tested. In the tests of advertising claims presented in these activities, the manipulated variable will be the particular brand. The responding variable will be whatever results are measured— the amount of water absorbed or how well stains are removed, for example. Everything else about the test, such as the amount of the product used, water temperature, and type of stain, should be identical for each brand. That way any difference observed in the results can be counted on to have been caused by the brand being used (the manipulated variable).

It's important to repeat every test at least three times. Anything that happens only once could simply be a freak occurrence. Repeating a test can be made easier by having everyone do a test once and then sharing the results.

Teaching Strategies

Set up a product testing center and stock it with all the things needed for performing the four product-claims tests. Ask students to bring in product samples for these tests. Have students tackle these tests in small groups and prepare them for performing these activities by presenting the background information on how to experiment using good scientific methods.

Allow plenty of time for the groups to share what they discover. Draw a class conclusion about the product claims. Have the groups prepare short summaries of their tests and conclusions and compile these into a class consumer guide to send home to parents as suggested in the extender activity.

Extenders

1. Wise Buys: Have students work in small groups to test other commercial claims, such as how well dishwashing soap cuts grease and how long a battery will last. Then have students prepare a class consumer guide to send home to parents.

Answers

Checking Out the Claims 1: The Paper Race: 1. Answers will vary but should include a difference in texture and size of holes created by the weave; 2. Answers will vary but should present logical reason to support prediction; 3. Answers will vary but should be based on results recorded on chart; 4. Answers will vary but should provide logical reason based on test. **2: That Tears It:** 1. Answers will vary but should include a difference in texture and size of holes created by the weave; 2. Answers will vary but should present logical reason to support prediction; 3. Answers will vary but should be based on results recorded on chart; 4. Answers will will vary but should provide logical reason based on test. **3: Suds and More Suds:** 1, 2. Answers will vary but should be logical, precise observations; 3. Answers will vary but should present logical reasons to support predictions; **4: Come Clean:** 1, 2. Answers will vary but should be logical, precise observations; 3. Answers will vary but should present logical reasons to support prediction; 4. With these variables controlled, you can be sure that any difference in stain removal was caused by the detergent; 5. Answers will vary but statement should clearly be a fact; 6. Answers will vary but statement should clearly express an opinion.

Using the Activities

Resources

How To Do A Science Project & Report by Martin J. Gutnik. New York: Franklin Watts, 1980.
The Young Scientist's Guide To Successful Science Projects by Sandra Markle. New York: Lothrop, Lee & Shepard, 1990).

Fact or Opinion?
(p. 19)
Thirst Quencher
(p. 20)
Hot Dog?
(p. 21)
Smart Shopper
(p. 22)

Supplies

A copy of each of the worksheets for each child.

Background Information

While advertisements most often present opinions, they may also offer facts that can help consumers decide which product to buy or even whether to make a purchase. Facts are statistics based on scientific research. These are most often presented in the form of numbers. Key words, such as *preferred* and *favorite*, reveal that what's being presented is only an opinion.

Reading labels is an important part of evaluating a product, particularly a food item. Labels tell what a product is made of. On a food product, the ingredients are listed in order so that the first three items represent the main ingredients. For example, a fruit drink that has fruit juice listed third after water and sucrose (a form of sugar) probably won't provide much nourishing fruit juice. Labels must also list amounts of vitamins, minerals, and additives, such as preservatives.

Teaching Strategies

Set up a center for performing these activities. Have students bring in clean, empty juice and drink cans, boxes, and bottles to be used when performing the Thirst Quencher activity. To conserve materials, present the Hot Dog? activity as a demonstration. Have students perform the Smart Shopper worksheet as a take-home activity. Allow time for students to share their results.

Extenders

1. A Real Bargain: Compile a class set of guidelines to use in determining whether something on sale is really the best buy.
2. Eye Buy: Have students make a list of which products are at eye level in each of these areas of the grocery store: cereal, ice cream, jelly. Discuss what effect shelf position might have on sales. Next, have students bring in a selection of empty cereal boxes. Compare the packages. Compile a class list of ways manufacturers use packaging to sell their products (discount prices, prize offers, eye-catching colors, commercial claims, for example).

Answers

Fact or Opinion?: 1. O, 2. F, 3. F, 4. F, 5. O, 6. O, 7. F, 8. F; **Thirst Quencher:** 2. Answers will vary; 3. Answers will vary but choice should be based on the results recorded on the chart; 4. Juices contain much more real juice and usually have much less added sugar; **Hot Dog?:** 1–3. Answers will vary depending on products studied; 4. Answers will vary but should show careful measuring; **Smart Shopper:** 1–7 Answers will vary; 8. Answers will vary but should present logical reason based on product analysis.

Resources

Be a Smart Shopper by Kathlyn Gay. Englewood Cliffs, New Jersey: Messner, 1974.
The School on Madison Avenue: Advertising and What It Teaches by Ann E. Weiss. New York: E.P. Dutton, 1980.

Investigating Change

Teachers' Notes

Getting Started

Investigating change provides students with opportunities to think creatively and tackle problem-solving situations. To start kids thinking, divide the class into small groups and give each group an ice cube in a self-sealing plastic bag. Have the groups observe how the ice cube changes as it melts and discuss together what conditions affect how quickly the ice melts.

Next, challenge your students to figure out a way to keep an ice cube from melting for the longest possible period of time. Allow time for the groups to brainstorm and plan how they'll tackle this problem. Then pass out fresh ice cubes in self-sealing plastic bags. Have each group quickly measure the length and width of its cube and record this information. After five minutes of following their plans to prevent melting, the groups should remeasure their cubes. (Or you could have the students weigh their cubes on a kitchen scale before starting, drain off any water after the time limit is up, and reweigh them.)

Allow time for the groups to share their results. Discuss as a class which techniques were the most effective for preserving the ice cubes. Draw a class conclusion, based on what was discovered, and ask what might be even more effective. Encourage students to test this method at home and report back to the class.

Bulletin Board Ideas

1. Inventors and Inventions: Turn your bulletin board into a challenging quiz with the questions listed below. To make this interactive activity self-checking, fold sheets of paper in half lengthwise. Write the questions on the front and the answers on the inside. Or post the answers somewhere else in the classroom.

1. Who invented the first phonograph as one of his 1,093 inventions? (*Thomas Edison*)
2. King Gillette wanted to invent something that people would use once and then throw away—so he could sell them another one. What did he invent? (*disposable razor blade*)
3. George de Mestral was inspired to invent this new kind of fastener after picking burrs off his dog. What did he invent? (*Velcro*)
4. Who invented the telephone? (*Alexander Graham Bell*)
5. David Bushnell went to great depths for his invention. What did he invent? (*first successful submarine*)
6. Jack Kilby's invention was tiny, but that's why it created such a huge change. What did Kilby invent? (*The first integrated circuit, more commonly called the chip*)
7. Chester Greenwood's cold ears led to an invention that made him famous. What did he invent? (*earmuffs*)
8. Walter Morrison got an idea for his invention by watching people play catch with an empty pie pan. What did he invent? (*the Frisbee*)

2. You've Come a Long Way, Baby: Looking at baby pictures can be a lot of fun when the baby has grown up into a familiar adult. Collect childhood photos from adults your students know well, such as the principal, librarian, cafeteria workers, and janitor. Don't forget one of yourself. Display these, attractively mounted, with a challenge to figure out who's who. If possible, display current pictures for matching. Allow guessing to continue while students investigate changes. Then reveal the identities of the now-famous babies.

Note: Some of the experiments in this unit require students to average results. You may want to review averaging with your class.

Name: _____

It'll Grow on You............

Directions: Follow the steps below to get started. Then answer the questions as you watch for changes.

- Place three to five charcoal briquettes in an aluminum pie pan.

- Mix together one-quarter cup salt, one-quarter cup laundry bluing, and one tablespoon of ammonia. Then stir in one-quarter cup water.

- Pour the solution over the briquettes. For a special effect, sprinkle drops of food coloring over the briquettes.

1. Record the date and time that you begin this investigation.

Check frequently until you first observe some tiny crystals. How long did it take for this

first change to appear? _____

_____

2. Use a magnifying glass to examine the first crystals. Describe what they look like.

_____

_____

3. Check again one hour later. In what ways, if any, have the crystals changed? _____

_____

_____

4. Check twice a day until the crystals no longer appear to be spreading or growing.

How many days did it take for the crystals to finish growing? _____

Name: _____

Quick Change..........................

Directions: Now that you've observed crystals growing, see if you can figure out how to produce crystals even faster.

1. Think of all the things that might have affected how quickly crystals formed. List everything you think might speed up crystal growth.

_____

_____

_____

_____

2. Next, think about which of your ideas would be too difficult or too expensive to try. Then list the one practical idea you think is your best chance to speed up crystal growth. _____

Why did you choose this idea?_____

_____

3. Set up a new crystal solution exactly as you did the first time, making only the change you chose in No. 2. Why is it important to keep everything else in the experiment the same?_____

_____

4. Check this new solution frequently, watching for the first crystals. Did they grow faster this time?   ☐ Yes ☐ No

How much faster or slower did the crystals form?

_____

_____

Name: _____

Getting Your Money's Worth...

Will you be able to squeeze more plain water or more soapy water onto the head of a quarter before it overflows?

Directions: Follow the steps below to examine how soap changes water. Next, predict whether you'll be able to get more drops of plain or soapy water onto the head of a quarter. Then test your prediction. You'll need water, a quarter, waxed paper, a toothpick dipped in liquid detergent, and an eyedropper.

1. Sprinkle several drops of water onto a sheet of waxed paper. Describe the shape of the

drops. _____

2. Now, touch one of the drops with a soapy toothpick. Describe how the drop has changed.

_____

3. Do you think a quarter will hold more plain water or more soapy water?_____

Why? _____

Number of Drops on a Quarter

Water	Test 1	Test 2	Test 3	Average
Plain				
Soapy				

4. What did you discover when you tested your predictions? _____

_____

5. Why was it important to perform each test three times and average the results? _____

_____

Save That Bubble

Exposed to room-temperature air, a soap bubble will gradually become drier and drier. And as it dries, the soap film surrounding a balloon of air becomes thinner and thinner until...POP!

Directions: Your challenge is to make a soap bubble last as long as possible. Amazing as it may seem, one record-making bubble didn't burst for 340 days—almost a year. You'll need one-half cup of the Super Bubble Solution your teacher has prepared for you, a clean plastic straw, and whatever items are required to test the three methods you select for preserving a soap bubble.

1. List everything you can think of that could affect how quickly a soap bubble dries.

_____

_____

2. Now, spend two minutes thinking of everything you could do to keep a bubble from

drying. List your ideas here*: _____

_____

3. What variables (things you can change) will you need to control as you test your

bubble-saving methods? _____

4. Complete the chart as you test the three ideas you think will be most successful.
Repeat each test three times.

Time Bubble Lasts (seconds)

Method	Test 1	Test 2	Test 3	Average Time

5. Which method worked best? _____

Why do you think it was the most successful? _____

* Use the back of this page if you need more room.

Name: _____

More Than Wet..........................

How is salt water different from fresh water?

Directions: Fill a quart jar with tap water. Prepare a jar of salt water following the recipe listed below. Then perform the investigation to find out.

> ### Salt Water
>
> 1. Pour one-half cup table salt into a clear glass quart jar.
> 2. Add three cups of hot tap water.
> 3. Stir until the salt is completely dissolved.
> 4. Allow to cool to room temperature.

1. Pour one-quarter cup of the salt water solution into a clear plastic cup. Pour one-quarter cup of tap water into a second plastic cup. Compare the two solutions using each of these senses. Tell how the salt water differs from the tap water.

Sight: _____

Smell: _____

Taste (take a small sip): _____

Touch: _____

2. Slip a hard-boiled egg into the jar of salt water and one into the jar of tap water. Observe what happens to each egg. Which do you think is denser (thicker)?

☐ Salt water   ☐ Tap water

Why? _____

Name:_____

You've Changed·····················

Directions: Put a baby picture of yourself in the frame below. Then answer the questions:

┌───┐
│   │
│   │
│   │
│   │
│   │
│   │
│   │
└───┘

1. List at least five ways you've changed since that picture was taken.

_____

_____

_____

2. What's something you can do well now that you couldn't do then?

_____

3. Is there anything about yourself that you wish hadn't changed as you got older?

_____

4. What about yourself do you most want to change in the future?

_____

Growing Up···························

Directions: Use books and encyclopedias to help you describe how each of these animals changes as it grows up.

1. Dog: _____

_____

2. Deer: _____

_____

3. Eagle: _____

_____

4. Kangaroo: _____

_____

5. Butterfly: _____

_____

Number the pictures to show the way a frog changes as it develops into an adult.

   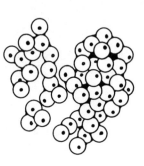

_____   _____   _____   _____

Name: _____

The Big Chew........................

How does chewing a piece of chewing gum change it?

Directions: Follow the steps below, recording your observations on the chart. You'll need a stick of chewing gum, a tape measure, and a kitchen scale.

- Unwrap the gum and lay it on its wrapper. Then examine the gum using all your senses. Also weigh and measure it.

- Put the stick of gum in your mouth and chew it fifty times.

- Then take the gum out of your mouth and put it back on the wrapper. Examine, measure, and weigh the gum again.

Observations

	Before Chewing	After Chewing
Sight:		
Touch:		
Smell:		
Length:		
Width:		
Weight:		

1. What was the most dramatic way the gum changed after it was chewed?

_____

_____

2. In what way did chewing affect the gum least? _____

_____

This Food's for You.............

You can't witness all the changes that food goes through as your digestive system breaks it down to fuel your body's growth and actions. But you can observe how foods begin to change in your mouth.

Directions: Answer the questions as you perform the investigation below.

1. Put a bite-size soda cracker in your mouth. Don't chew. Hold it in your mouth for thirty seconds. Describe how the cracker tastes. _____

_____

2. How does your mouth feel as the thirty-second limit approaches?

☐ Moister   ☐ Drier

3. Enzymes are special chemicals produced by your body to break down the food you eat. Your saliva contains an enzyme that breaks down starches like those in the cracker, so the cracker should taste different than it did when you first put it in your mouth. What is the flavor like now?

☐ Sweeter   ☐ Less sweet

4. Feel the cracker with your tongue. Describe all the other ways the cracker has changed since you first put it in your mouth. _____

_____

Name: _____

Mirror Image ....

How is a mirror image different from the real thing?

Directions: Perform this investigation to find out. Then answer the questions.

- Have a friend stand beside a mirror facing you. Then stand in front of the mirror and ask your friend to copy exactly what you do. Touch your right cheek with your right hand. Wave your left hand.

- Write your name on a piece of paper. Hold it up and read it in the mirror.

1. How did your mirror image differ from what you could see your friend doing?

_____

_____

2. In what ways, if any, did the mirror image change the way your writing looked?

_____

_____

The famous Italian inventor and artist Leonardo da Vinci wrote notes on his experiments in mirror writing. Try writing a message in mirror writing. You've succeeded when the mirror image of your message looks like normal print. Then hold this paper up to a mirror to read the answer to this riddle:

What kind of beans will never grow in a garden?

ꙅnɒɘdʏllɘႱ

Mirror Image (Continued) ·····························

What kind of images are reflected in a curved mirror?

Directions: Perform this investigation and answer the questions to record what you find out.

3. Look at yourself in the bowl of a shiny metal spoon. How do you look?

☐ Upside down   ☐ Right side up

4. Next, look at yourself in the curved back of the shiny metal spoon. How do you look now?

☐ Upside down   ☐ Right side up

5. A mirror that curves in like the spoon bowl is called a *concave* mirror. A mirror that curves out like the back of a spoon is called a *convex* mirror. Look at your reflection in both kinds of curved mirrors again. Which one makes you look bigger?

☐ Concave   ☐ Convex

6. Which kind of mirror would you want to use in a fun house to make someone look tall and skinny?

☐ Convex   ☐ Concave

BONUS CHALLENGE ★★★★★★★

Mirrors can be an important tool. Tell how each of these professionals uses mirrors.

1. A truck driver: _____

2. A dentist: _____

3. A beautician: _____

4. An astronomer: _____

5. A submarine captain: _____

Name:_____

Gone Moldy........................

Does temperature affect how quickly bread molds?

Directions: Answer the questions as you perform the investigation to find out. You'll need two slices of fresh white bread; two self-sealing plastic sandwich bags; and two brown paper lunch sacks.

• Sprinkle both slices of bread with water. Then place each slice in a bag, seal the bags, and place each bag inside a lunch sack. Fold the tops of the lunch sacks closed.

• Place one bag in the refrigerator and set the other bag in a warm spot. Sprinkle with water as needed to keep the bread moist but not soggy.

1. What conditions must be kept the same for both slices of bread?

_____

_____

2. Check the bread daily. On which slice does fuzzy mold appear first?

_____

3. Keep checking. How many more days is it before mold begins to grow on the other

slice?_____

4. Describe all the ways that the mold changed the bread._____

_____

_____

_____

_____

The Shadow..............................

How does changing the position of a light source change the way a shadow looks?

Directions: Answer the questions as you perform the investigation to find out. You'll need a flashlight and a juice can. For best results work in a dark or dimly lit room.

1. Shine the flashlight at the can as shown in each of the pictures. Circle the test that produced the longest shadow.

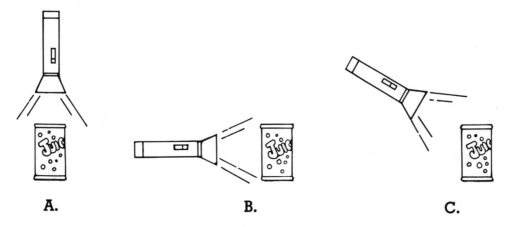

A.   B.   C.

2. Aim the flashlight at the can from as many angles as you can think of. Have a friend help you measure the longest shadow you can produce. How long is this shadow?____

3. Based on what you've discovered, what time of day do you think your own shadow will be longest outdoors?   ☐ 10:00 a.m.   ☐ Noon   ☐ 4:00 p.m.

4. Where is the light source that produced the shadow in this picture?

A. Aimed at an angle from the left side

B. Straight above the object

C. Aimed at an angle from the right side

Animals That Change Color

Directions: Think creatively as you tackle these colorful problems. Check in books and encyclopedias to find out more about these animals.

1. The chameleon, the octopus, and the flounder are all able to change their skin color and even the pattern of their coloration. How does this ability to change color help these animals survive?

_____

_____

_____

2. When a squid is frightened, it turns bright red. Why is this color change a good defense?

_____

_____

3. An octopus changes colors to express its emotions. It may be orange, red, or dark purple when it's angry or excited. When it's frightened, it turns black. When it's comfortable and at rest it's usually gray. What if your skin changed colors to express your emotions? List what color you think would best express each of these feelings:

Happiness: _____

Sadness: _____

Anger: _____

Fear:_____

4. When you blush, you make a quick color change. You can't stop a blush. It happens when blood rushes through blood vessels close to the surface of the skin. Blushing is usually an emotional response. Describe something that makes you blush.

_____

_____

_____

Name:_____

Getting Ready for Winter...

Directions: Use books and encyclopedias to find out how each of these animals prepares for winter.

1. Arctic Tern: _____

_____

2. Black Bear: _____

_____

3. Green Frog: _____

_____

4. Monarch Butterfly:_____

_____

5. Snowshoe Hare: _____

_____

BONUS CHALLENGE ★★★★★★★

List all the things you can think of that people do to get ready for winter.

_____

_____

_____

_____

_____

Name:_____

Different As Day and Night

Directions: Perform the tests below and observe carefully to discover how night really is different from day. Then answer the questions.

1. On a bright, sunny day, watch the sky as the sun sets. List all the different colors you

observe in the order they appear._____

_____

2. Describe all the ways that a clear, nighttime sky looks different from a clear daytime

sky. _____

_____

3. Check and record the air temperature at each of these times.

2:00 p.m._____

4:00 p.m._____

6:00 p.m._____

8:00 p.m._____

4. How did the temperature change as day became night? _____

Why do you think this happened?_____

_____

5. At about 2:00 in the afternoon and again about an hour after dark, go outdoors and
listen carefully for one minute. Describe what you hear.

Daytime: _____

_____

Nighttime: _____

_____

Plane Tactics..............................

Directions: First, follow the steps below to build and fly a straw plane. Then, figure out a way to change your plane to make it fly even farther. Test the success of your new design. You'll need scissors, tape, and a plastic straw.

- Cut out the paper strips at the bottom of the page. Use tape to hook the ends of the shorter strip together to form a loop. Do the same thing with the longer strip. Next, attach the loops to the straw as shown, taping them in place.

- Stand at a starting mark on the flight range your teacher has set up for you. Throw your plane with the smaller loop aimed forward. Measure how far the plane traveled before it stopped and record that on the Flight Data Chart on the next page. Test your plane two more times and record the flight distance. Then compute the average distance your plane flew.

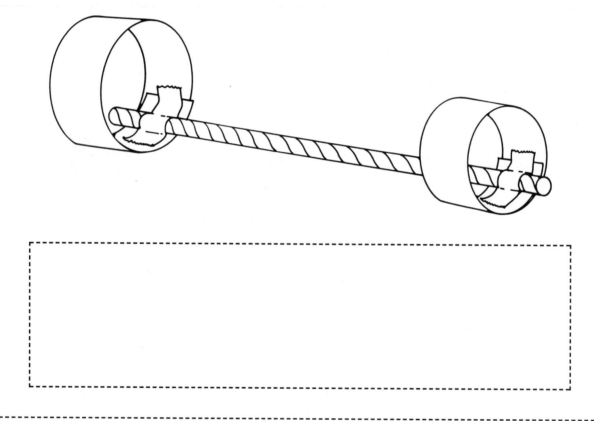

Name:_____

Plane Tactics (Continued) ....

FLIGHT DATA CHART

Plane Design   **Distance traveled**

	Test 1	Test 2	Test 3	Average
Basic:				
Change 1:				
Change 2:				
Change 3:				

1. List all the changes you can think of to make your plane fly even farther.

_____

_____

_____

_____

Pick the three changes you think will be most successful and write these on the chart above.

2. In order to tell how each change affects the plane's flight, you'll need to keep everything (except what you changed) the same in all the tests. What will you need to keep the same?

_____

_____

3. Now change the plane in one of the ways you chose. Test it three times, record the results on the chart and compute an average. Then change the plane in each of the other ways you chose and make three test flights. Why is it important to try each plane design three times and then compute an average? _____

4. Based on your most successful change, how do you think you could improve the plane even more?_____

_____

Name: _____

Rings a Bell ....

Will changing the amount of water in a quart jar change the sound?

Directions: Answer the questions as you perform the investigation to find out. You'll need four identical glass quart jars, a measuring cup, water, and a metal spoon.

- Fill the jars to make the water levels match the pictures below. Then use the spoon to strike the side of jars one, two and three in turn.

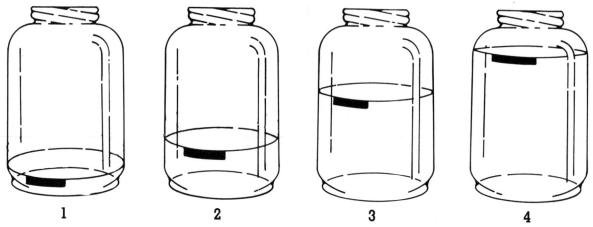

| 1 | 2 | 3 | 4 |

1. Based on what you discovered, do you think the sound produced by jar 4 will be higher or

lower than jar 3? _____ Why?_____

2. Adjust the amount of water in the four jars until you can use them to play a scale. Then use measuring cups and spoons to measure exactly how much water is in each jar. List the amount in each jar.

Jar 1: _____   Jar 3: _____

Jar 2: _____   Jar 4: _____

BONUS CHALLENGE ★★★★★★★   If you blow across the top of an empty glass bottle, you'll produce a deep tone. But if you strike the side of that same bottle, you'll produce a high tone. How can the same bottle produce two such different sounds?

_____

_____

Name: _____

New and Improved............

Directions: Inventors often simply develop improvements for products that already exist. Choose one of the items from the list below. Then follow the steps to decide how you would improve that product.

Can opener
Toothbrush
Paper cup
Bicycle pump

Umbrella
Automatic dishwasher
Automatic clothes dryer
Juice can

Tennis shoes
Soap dispenser
Backpack
Fingernail clippers

1. Which product have you selected to improve? _____

2. What one feature about this product would you want to keep the same?

_____

3. Describe all the ways you think this product could be improved. _____

_____

_____

_____

4. What change do you think would make people eager to buy your improved product?

_____

_____

On the back of this page, write a commercial that could be used on the radio to advertise your newly improved product.

It'll Grow on You
(p. 28)
Quick Change
(p. 29)

Supplies

A copy of each of the worksheets for each child. To complete the It'll Grow on You activity, each group will need three to five charcoal briquettes, an aluminum pie pan, a measuring cup, measuring spoons, one-quarter cup salt, one-quarter cup laundry bluing, one-quarter cup water, and one tablespoon of ammonia (food coloring optional). To complete the Quick Change activity, each group needs the materials used in It'll Grow on You.

Background Information

Crystals form when the liquid material in this investigation changes to a solid. This simulates to some extent how minerals form crystals from molten material in the earth's crust. The slower the mineral material cools, allowing time for crystal growth, the bigger the developing crystals will become. If there is plenty of room for them to develop, crystals of specific kinds of minerals will take characteristic shapes. Salt crystals, for example, are always cubes, and quartz crystals are always hexagonal. A crystal's shape depends on the mineral's unique atomic pattern.

The largest crystal ever discovered in the United States was a spodumene crystal 42 feet long, weighing about 90 tons. It was found in Etta Mine near Keystone, South Dakota. Some feldspar crystals found in the Soviet Union weighed thousands of tons each. The most valued crystals are diamonds.

Probably the most common crystals are ice crystals. These hexagonal crystals are more commonly called snowflakes.

Teaching Strategies

Have students work on the It'll Grow on You activity in small groups. Allow time for the groups to share their results. Then allow each group to tackle the problem-solving situation provided in the Quick Change activity. Next, compile a class list of possible variables to be changed and have each group select a different variable to test. Then have the groups compare their results and draw a class conclusion about which produced the fastest-growing crystals. To keep the action going, full-grown crystal gardens may be sprayed with water to dissolve the crystals and start them growing again. Sticking toothpicks in the gardens will create artistic spires.

Extenders

1. Watch It Grow: Perform this demonstration to let your students observe other crystals form. First, pour one-half cup Epsom salts into one cup of hot water and stir until completely dissolved. Next, pour just enough of this solution into a glass pie plate to cover the bottom. Let the pie plate sit, and have students check frequently for signs of crystal growth. As the liquid evaporates, frostlike crystals will form. When no more liquid remains, the crystals are completely formed. Have students hold the plate up to a light to examine the crystal structure. To show students what happens to a crystal structure if the solution hardens very quickly instead of slowly, freeze a second batch of the solution and have students compare the results. There will be no obvious crystals in the frozen solution. If possible, display a piece of obsidian. This natural glass forms when molten material cools very quickly. It looks smooth and clear because, as in the frozen Epsom salts solution, crystals didn't have time to form.

2. Cold Crystals: If you live where it snows, have your students bundle up and go outside for a snowflake hunt. Have students work as partners, taking along magnifying glasses and pieces of black paper to catch the ice crystals for a closer look. Tell students to hold the paper by the edge rather than flat across the palm, to avoid breathing on the flakes, and to expect to get only a quick look.

Answers

It'll Grow on You: 1. Answers will vary, but it shouldn't take more than a few hours for the crystals to first appear; 2. Descriptions will vary but should mention feathery shape, delicate structure, and many tiny points; 3. Answers will vary but should include becoming larger and developing more points; 4. Answers will vary, but growth should be complete within a couple of days.

Quick Change: 1. Answers will vary but should include ways to speed up evaporation of the crystal-forming solution ; 2. Answers will vary but should be logical and supported by sound reasoning; 3. That way you can be sure that the crystal's forming faster was caused by what you changed; 4. Answers will vary.

Resources

Album of Rocks and Minerals by Tom McHowen. New York: Macmillan, 1981.
Crystals by Philip B. Carona. Chicago: Follett Publishing Company, 1971.
Digging Deeper: Investigations into Rocks, Shocks, Quakes, and Other Earthy Matters by Sandra

Using the Activities ·····················

Markle. New York: Lothrop, Lee & Shepard, 1987.

Getting Your Money's Worth
(p. 30)
Save That Bubble
(p. 31)
More Than Wet
(p. 32)

Supplies

A copy of each of the worksheets for each child. To perform the Getting Your Money's Worth activity, each child will need a sheet of waxed paper, water, a toothpick that has been dipped in liquid detergent, a quarter, and an eyedropper.

To complete the Save That Bubble activity, students will need one-half cup of Super Bubble Solution and a plastic straw. To mix the Super Bubble Solution combine one part liquid dishwashing detergent (without any scent or other special additives), two parts glycerin (available at grocery stores), and three parts water. To perform the More Than Wet activity, groups will need a measuring cup, table salt, a long-handled spoon, water, a hard-boiled egg, 2 clear plastic cups, and 2 clear glass quart jars.

Background Information

Each water molecule is made up of two atoms of hydrogen and one atom of oxygen. The atoms of one molecule form bonds with those of other water molecules locking them tightly together. In fact, this bonding creates a surface tension that is like the film on water. It's also why a water drop has a dome shape. The molecules resist the downward pull of gravity, which would spread out the drop and break their bonds. Touching a soapy toothpick to a drop of water, though, makes the drop flatten into a puddle. Soap molecules break the bonds between water molecules. A water molecule then attaches to one end of a soap molecule. The other end of each soap molecule is free to attach to a particle of dirt. The soap molecule holds the dirt particle suspended in the water until this soap-dirt-water molecule is rinsed away with more water.

Many different substances dissolve in water. When they dissolve, they change the density or thickness of the water. Anyone who has ever been swimming in the ocean has discovered that it's easier to float in denser, salty water than in fresh water.

Teaching Strategies

These three activities may be combined to create a fun hands-on center. To provide a motivational starter, fill a pie plate about two-thirds full of water. As your students watch, sprinkle the surface with either pepper or a fine coating of talcum powder. Then dip a cotton-tipped swab into a liquid dishwashing detergent and touch the soapy tip to the very center of the water. The soap will break the water's skinlike surface tension and cause the floating particles to shoot away from the center toward the sides of the pie plate. After students have had an opportunity to investigate water's special characteristics through the activities, repeat this demonstration, guiding them to understand why this happened. Encourage your students to be creative as they test ideas for ways to make the bubbles last. Provide an ongoing test area for students involved in this research to share their results and to encourage the class to brainstorm additional innovative ways to make bubbles last.

Extenders

1. Bubble Challenge: Give each child a clean plastic straw and some of the Super Bubble Solution in a clear plastic cup. Challenge them to blow the biggest bubble. To measure a bubble, have the child let the bubble break against a sheet of paper and then measure the distance across the wet spot it creates. Or challenge them to blow the tallest bubble tower.
2. To Dissolve or Not: Encourage your students to discover materials that will dissolve in water. This could be set up as a center activity with a group of "mystery" matters to test. Or it could be a take-home activity designed to encourage creative thinking. Allow time for students to share what they discovered and compile a class list. You may also want to have students investigate whether materials dissolve faster in hot water than they do in cold water. (They do.)

Answers

Getting Your Money's Worth: 1. The drops will be round and dome-shaped; 2. The drops flatten and spread out, taking on an irregular shape; 3. Predictions will vary but should be supported by logical reasons; 4. Answers will vary; 5. The result of one test could be a freak occurrence. **Save That Bubble:** 1. Students will undoubtedly think of additional variables, but the list should include air temperature, wind speed, and the amount of humidity in the air; 2. Answers will vary; 3. Students should say that everything needs to be kept the same except the method being tested. The things to be kept the same should include air temperature, wind speed, and exposure to light;

49

4. Test methods and results will vary; 5. Answers will vary, but a supportive reason should show logical thought. **More Than Wet:** 1. Sight—salt water will be cloudier; smell—salt water will have a distinctly salty smell; taste—salt water will have a salty taste; touch—salt water will feel different—may be sticky or slippery; 2. Salt water, because the egg floats in the salt water and sinks in the tap water.

Resources

Water: Experiments to Understand It by Boris Arnov. New York: Lothrop, Lee & Shepard, 1980.
A Children's Museum Activity Book: Bubbles by Bernie Zubrowski. Boston: Little, Brown, 1979.
Bubbles and Bubble Blowers by the editors of Green Tiger Press. San Diego, CA: Green Tiger Press, 1982.

You've Changed
(p. 33)
Growing Up
(p. 34)

Supplies

A copy of each of the worksheets for each child.

Background Information

Some baby animals, such as alligators and snakes, begin life looking like small versions of the adults and are basically able to take care of themselves. Other baby animals, such as birds and humans, are helpless and need extensive care by adults. Some of the babies that start out helpless grow up very fast. Arctic hares, for example, must mature quickly in order to be strong enough to survive the harsh arctic winters. So these youngsters are able to

hop about within a couple of days and no longer need their mother's milk within two weeks. Human babies, on the other hand, require nurturing for many years.

Some baby animals change form completely as they mature. Frogs start out as tadpoles, which have tails and no legs and can live only in water. Then the tadpole gradually loses its tail and develops legs, and loses its gills and develops lungs. Butterflies are another example of an animal that goes through a complete change. The young hatches as a caterpillar. Later, it forms a chrysalis about itself. After another period of growth, the adult emerges as a butterfly.

Teaching Strategies

Begin by having students perform the You've Changed worksheet as a take-home activity and allow time for them to share their answers. Then display these sheets for everyone to enjoy the pictures of classmates when they were much younger. You may even want to select a few to display with the question "Can you guess who this is?"

If possible, arrange for a parent to bring in a baby animal for a brief visit as a motivational starter for the Growing Up activity. Allow time for students to share what they discovered while completing this activity.

Extenders

1. Right Before Their Eyes: Many frogs and toads lay their eggs between March and May. If you discover some, scoop them up, along with pond water, in a self-sealing plastic bag . If possible, collect some green pond scum to supply food. Back in the classroom, transfer the eggs,

water, and plants to a small fishbowl or a clean quart jar. If the eggs are in long tubes or strings, they're probably toad eggs. Frog eggs are usually in clusters.

As soon as the tadpoles hatch, transfer them to a larger container filled with pond water or tap water that has been allowed to sit for several days. If you run out of natural food, add a few pieces of boiled lettuce. Change the water every few days and keep the container out of direct sunlight.

When the tadpoles sprout hind legs, add rocks and gravel so the young adults can climb out of the water. Put a screen over the top so your visitors won't hop out. They'll also need a new diet—mealworms or small insects. After the transformation to adulthood is complete, return the frogs or toads to their home pond.

Answers

You've Changed: 1. Answers will vary but should include getting taller, stronger, and possibly having more hair, freckles, etc.; 2. Answers will vary but should express increased ability to do things independently; 3, 4. Answers will vary but should express creative thought.
Growing Up: 1. A puppy is smaller than an adult dog, has softer or even slightly different-colored hair, and its eyes are closed for a short time after birth. A puppy is also weaker, less coordinated, and has baby teeth. 2. A fawn has spots to provide camouflage. It also lacks the adult's distinct odor so its scent will not attract predators; 3. An eaglet's feathers at first are soft and downy, and the young birds can't fly. First adult feathers are all dark, and eyes are also dark;

4. A joey is tiny, naked, and helpless when it's born. Its eyes are closed. The joey crawls into its mother's pouch and remains there, sucking on a nipple, for about five months as it grows larger, develops hair, and opens its eyes; 5. A butterfly goes through a complete change. A wormlike caterpillar hatches from the egg. Later, this becomes a resting pupal stage, and from this, the adult winged butterfly emerges; Frog life cycle: 3,4,2,1.

Resources

Animal Babies by Bobbie Hamsa. Chicago: Children's Press, 1985. *Baby Animals* by Illa Podendorf. Chicago: Children's Press, 1981. *Birth and Growth: The Human Body* by Brian R. Ward. New York: Franklin Watts, 1983.

The Big Chew
(p. 35)
This Food's for You
(p. 36)

Supplies

A copy of each of the worksheets for each child. To perform the Big Chew activity, each child will need a stick of chewing gum plus access to a tape measure and a kitchen scale. To complete the This Food's for You activity, each student will need a soda cracker.

Background Information

Digestion begins as soon as you put food in your mouth. As you chew, your teeth, tongue, and cheek muscles work together to grind and mix the food with saliva, a liquid containing an enzyme that starts breaking down food. The body produces about 700 different enzymes to chemically break down food. *Amylase*, the one in saliva, begins to break starch into sugar.

Saliva also moistens food to make it easier to swallow and help you taste food.

Muscular action carries food through the rest of the digestive system. Food is squeezed down the esophagus at the rate of about two inches per second. In the stomach, waves of muscular action, called *peristalsis*, continue to push food through the digestive system. Strong acid and more enzymes also attack food in the stomach. Stomach acid is neutralized when the partly digested food moves into the small intestine.

The enzymes produced by the pancreas and the liver finish chemically breaking food into nutrient particles. These nutrients pass through finger-like projections called *villi*, which line the small intestine. There they enter capillaries and are carried by the bloodstream to the body's cells.

Teaching Strategies

Have students work in small groups with each person in the group performing the activity but all combining their observations. Allow time for the groups to share what they discovered about how chewing affects the gum. Then have students perform the This Food's for You activity to continue exploring digestion. Share the background information. Follow this by having students perform the You Are What You Eat extender activity.

Extenders

1. You Are What You Eat: Tell your students that they need to eat a specific amount of each of the six essential food nutrients— protein, carbohydrates, fats, water, vitamins, and minerals— every day. Because it's hard to know how much or even which of these essential nutrients are in

food, though, nutritionists have developed this formula for healthy eating: 4-4-3-2. Explain that this means eating four servings from the fruits-and-vegetables group, four servings from the breads-and-cereals group, three servings from the milk-yogurt-and-cheese group, and two servings from the meat-egg-nut-and-bean group. Next, have students keep track of everything they eat for one day, computing how many servings from each food group they ate. And have them make a list of snacks that could contribute to a day's worth of healthy eating.

2. What's in It?: Explain that ingredients are listed on a can's label in descending order of quantity, with the first three showing most of what that food contains. Have students bring in clean, empty cans to set up a center activity. Or have them explore at home or at their local supermarket. Challenge them to compare several brands of the same kind of chicken soup to see which is most likely to contain more meat. Or have them check the amount of sugar added to various brands of cereal. Tell students that sugar may have other names, such as sucrose and fructose. Allow time for students to share what they discover.

Answers

The Big Chew: 1. Should express a change in its shape; 2. Answers will vary and will depend on the type of gum. Beige to gray gums will have very little color change. Some students may find that the way the gum feels is the least changed. **This Food's for You:** 1. Answers will vary but should not taste sweet at first; 2. Moister; 3. Sweeter; 4. Answers will vary but should include softer, wetter, and more pulpy.

Resources

Eating by John Gaskin. New York: Franklin Watts, 1984.
Food and Digestion by Brian R. Ward. New York: Franklin Watts, 1983.
What Happens to a Hamburger by Paul Showers. New York: Thomas Y. Crowell, 1970.

Mirror Image
(pp. 37–38)

Supplies

A copy of the worksheet for each child. Students will also need a hand mirror, a partner, and a shiny metal spoon.

Background Information

Light generally travels in a straight line. All objects that don't give off their own light are visible because they reflect light, or bounce it back toward its source. The moon is visible because it reflects sunlight. Some objects reflect light better than others. Shiny, smooth objects reflect light best. A mirror is made by spraying a thin layer of shiny silver or aluminum onto a piece of very smooth glass.

Curved mirrors change the way a reflected image looks. A convex mirror curves out. This type of mirror makes images appear smaller than normal but right side up. If the image reflected by this type of mirror is beyond its focus point, however, the image may appear smaller than normal and upside down.

Teaching Strategies

Set up the Mirror Image activity as a center. Include the extender activities. Encourage your students to add to a class list of all the objects they can find that act like a mirror. Just for fun, post messages or riddles in mirror writing.

Extenders

1. Odd Images: Put two small, identical, rectangular hand mirrors out at a center. Have students stand these up with one edge touching and lay a pencil or another object between the mirrors. Challenge them to see how many reflections of an image they can make by changing the position of the mirrors. Allow time for students to share what they discover.
2. Reflected Art: Have students try to draw a picture of something while looking only at its reflection in a mirror. Discuss what makes this task difficult.

Answers

1. What is viewed in the mirror appears to be just the opposite of what the person is actually doing; 2. The mirror writing looks backward; 3. Upside down; 4. Right side up; 5. Concave; 6. Convex; Bonus Challenge: 1. To see cars behind him or her while looking straight ahead; 2. To see back teeth; 3. To show customers the back of their heads; 4. To reflect light from distant stars; 5. To reflect light from the surface to viewing point under water.

Resources

Reflections by Angela Webb. New York: Franklin Watts, 1988.
Light by Brenda Walpol. New York: Warwick Press, 1987.
Light Fantastic by Philip Watson. New York: Lothrop, Lee & Shepard, 1982.

Gone Moldy
(p. 39)

Supplies

A copy of the worksheet for each child. Each group will also need two slices of fresh white bread; two self-sealing, plastic sandwich bags; and two brown paper lunch sacks.

Background Information

Green plants are the beginning of all food chains, and fungi are the end. Fungi receive nourishment by dissolving other plant or animal tissues. They act like recyclers, decomposing dead insects, fallen leaves, and decaying food. Without them, the earth would be piled deep with garbage.

Instead of growing from seeds, fungi grow from tiny spores. Unlike seeds, which have a built-in supply of stored food to get the young plant started, a spore must land on a spot where there is an immediate food supply. The spot where the spore lands must also be warm and moist. Because these requirements make it harder for a fungus plant to grow, fungi produce millions, even billions of tiny spores.

Bread mold is a kind of fungus. The fuzzy spots are really threadlike structures that act as roots and stems. When these spots appear black, the threads have developed spore-producing bodies.

Teaching Strategies

Have students work on this activity in small groups or, to conserve materials, present this as a demonstration. If groups do perform the activity, allow time for students to share what they discover.

If you grow bread mold as a demonstration, have each student observe and answer the questions on his or her own. Then discuss the results as a class. Share the background information and have groups choose one of the fungi listed in the Check It Out extender to

Using the Activities ······················

research and make a report. Perform the Feeding Fungus extender as a demonstration.

Extenders

1. Feeding Fungus: Explain that yeast is a helpful fungus used to make bread dough rise. Demonstrate what happens as yeast grows by mixing together one package of dry yeast, one cup warm water, and one tablespoon of sugar in a clear plastic cup. Place this cup in a warm spot where your students can observe it. Within a short time, a thick foam will begin to form. Explain that the yeast plant is growing and as it grows it gives off carbon dioxide gas. Encourage your students to think about how the growing yeast would affect bread dough. Challenge your students to design an experiment to find out if the yeast plants need sugar in order to grow. (The cup containing the sugar and yeast will nearly overflow with foam.)

2. Check It Out: Have students work together in small groups, using books and encyclopedias to find out more about one of these fungi: mushrooms, rusts, "athlete's foot," smuts, powdery mildews, yeast, and penicillin. Allow time for the groups to share what they discover.

Answers

1. Other variables may be listed, but these conditions should be included: type of bread, size of slices, size of bag, amount of water, and exposure to light; 2. Should appear on the warmer slice first; 3. Should take a lot longer for mold to appear on the slice kept in the refrigerator; 4. Descriptions will vary but should include that moldy bread has spots of a different color, looks fuzzy, and may look flatter.

Resources

Lots of Rot by Vicki Cobb. Philadelphia: J.B. Lippincott, 1981. *Mushrooms and Molds* by Robert Froman. New York: Crowell Junior Books, 1972.

The Shadow
(p. 40)

Supplies

A copy of the worksheet for each child. To perform this activity, students will also need a flashlight, a juice can, and a dimly lit room. (A table could be draped with a blanket to create a dimly lit nook for this activity.)

Background Information

A shadow is formed when something blocks light from reaching a surface. The blocked area that appears dark is the shadow. The position of the shadow depends on the position of the light source; the shadow is always directly opposite its light source. When the light source is directly overhead, the shadow is short and fat. When the light source is at an angle, the shadow stretches out long and thin. Shadows provide important clues that help identify the shape and texture of objects. Ancient people used a kind of shadow clock called a sundial to tell time.

Teaching Strategies

Launch this activity with a game of shadow tag. This is played like regular tag only the person who is It tags by stepping on the other person's shadow.

Set The Shadow activity up as a center. Include the Bright World extender activity. Allow time for students to share their results and ideas. Post a class graph for the Timely Shadow

extender activity and let students take turns recording this data.

Extenders

1. Timely Shadows: Perform this demonstration to show how shadows change as the position of the sun changes during the day. Fill an empty can full of sand and stand a ruler up in it. Just after school starts on a sunny day, set this can outdoors and have a student draw around the ruler's shadow with colored chalk. On a piece of paper, keep a record of the time and the color of chalk used. Repeat this every two hours, having different students outline the shadow with different colors of chalk. Just before the end of the school day, compare the shadow outlines. If possible, take a photograph of the shadow outlines for the bulletin board.

2. Bright World: Challenge your students to imagine a shadowless world. What would they miss most about losing their own shadow? Could "erasing" shadows cause any problems? Allow time for students to share their ideas.

Answers

1.B.; 2. Answers will vary; 3. 4:00 p.m.; 4. C.

Resources

Light & Dark by Seymour Simon. New York: McGraw Hill, 1970. *Shadows: Here, There, and Everywhere* by Ron and Nancy Goor. New York: Thomas Y. Crowell, 1981. *Sun And Light* by Neil Ardley. New York: Franklin Watts, 1983.

53

Animals That Change Color
(p. 41)

Supplies

A copy of the worksheet for each child.

Background Information

A chameleon can change color quickly because of the complex arrangement of pigments in its skin. Different layers of skin are colored separately. One layer has only blue pigment. Another layer has only yellow pigment. In between these fixed color cells, there are special cells called *melanophores*. These blossom- or star-shaped cells contain dark pigment granules called *melanin*. Think of the melanin granules as grains of sand. The melanin can collect in a cluster in the cell's center or scatter throughout the cell. What color the chameleon appears depends on how the melanin granules are arranged. The more the dark granules spread out, the more they mask the layers of fixed colors. Melanin movement is controlled both by the chameleon's reaction to its environment and by its emotions. A quiet, happy chameleon is green or dull brown. An angry or excited chameleon becomes brown with light-yellow stripes and black spots.

An octopus is an artist at showing colorful feelings. Normally a neutral gray, this animal changes to deep rose, orange, red, or purple when it's excited or angry. These colors may blush over the animal in waves as it hunts and eats. The octopus can also make its coloring blend in with its surroundings. It can even be different colors on opposite sides of its body.

Teaching Strategies

Have students perform the Animals That Change Color activity as a take-home activity. Share the background information. Allow time for students to share their responses. Then have students work in small groups to creatively tackle the problem-solving situation presented in the Can You Spot It? extender activity.

Extenders

1. Can You Spot It? Use this activity to challenge your students to think creatively. First, show them an area indoors or outdoors. Next, have them create a make-believe animal that uses camouflage to be safe in that environment. Allow each student to "hide" the animal they created in plain sight. Then challenge the other students to find the hidden animals.

Answers

1. Makes them blend in with their environment so they are invisible to enemies; 2. Could frighten away an enemy; 3. Answers will vary but should express creativity; 4. Answers will vary

Resources

Animal and Plant Mimicry by Dorothy H. Patent. New York: Holiday House, 1978.
Chameleons and Other Quick-Change Artists by Hilda Simon. New York: Dodd, Mead & Company,1973.
Octopus by Carol Carrick. Boston: Clarion, 1978.

Getting Ready for Winter
(p. 42)

Supplies

A copy of the worksheet for each child.

Background Information

Animals prepare for winter in three main ways. Some, such as the Arctic tern and the monarch butterfly, travel to where it's warmer. Others, such as black bears and green frogs, spend the winter in a special kind of sleep called *hibernation*. When an animal hibernates, its heart rate and breathing rate are greatly reduced, and all body processes slow down so much that the animal can live off the food stored in its body. Some winter sleepers are really only nappers, waking up periodically to eat and then go back to sleep. Still others, such as the snowshoe rabbit, winterize by developing special features. This hardy bunny grows a white coat to camouflage it in the winter snow. It also grows tufts of long hair between its toes to help spread its already big feet into snowshoes.

Teaching Strategies

Have students tackle this library search in small groups. Share background information as students discuss what they discover. Compile a class list for the Bonus Challenge.

Extenders

1. Different World: Compile a class list of the ways in which winter differs from summer where you live. If you live where there is very little difference between the seasons, have your students explore what winter is like in a very different climate. If possible, have your class exchange letters with a class living where winter is very different than it is in your region.

Answers

1. Arctic tern migrates 11,000 miles from the Antarctic to islands

bordering the North Polar Basin; 2. Black bear hibernates, and during this time females give birth to cubs; 3. Green frog hibernates after burying itself; absorbs enough oxygen directly through skin to survive; 4. Monarch butterfly migrates, spending winter clinging to tree branches near Pacific Grove, California, or the mountains of Mexico; 5. Snowshoe rabbit develops special features as described in background information. Bonus Challenge: Answers will vary, but the list should include putting storm windows on house, putting antifreeze in cars, purchasing heavier clothes, and stocking up on food and fuel.

Resources

Animals That Migrate by Caroline Arnold. Minneapolis: Carolrhoda Books, 1982.
Animals In Winter by Romand M. Fisher. Washington, D.C.: National Geographic Society, 1982.
Exploring Winter by Sandra Markle. New York: Atheneum, 1984.

Different As Day and Night
(p. 43)

Supplies

A copy of the worksheet for each child.

Background Information

Whether it's day or night depends on the way the earth is turned. When the part of the earth you live on is turned toward the sun, it's day. And when that part of the earth is turned away from the sun, it's night. Besides the amount of visible light, one of the

main differences between day and night is temperature. Day is usually warmer. Most of the sunlight doesn't heat the earth's atmosphere directly though; land, water, plants, and even buildings absorb sunlight. Once it's absorbed, light energy changes to heat energy. Then all the warmed surfaces radiate heat, warming the air. Because some materials absorb more sunlight than others, the air above some areas is much warmer than others. Some surfaces, such as a bright, snow-covered field, for example, actually reflect away most of the light energy that reaches them.

Teaching Strategies

To launch this activity, ask students to consider what it would be like to live where the sun shines for most of the day and night during one part of the year and barely shines at all during another part of the year. What would they like about having this kind of extended day and night? What wouldn't they like about it? Next, have students perform this activity at home over a weekend. Encourage them to make careful, detailed observations and communicate what they discover using descriptive phrases and comparisons. Allow time for students to share their results. Present the background information about how sunlight heats the earth's atmosphere during the discussion of question No. 4.

Extenders

1. The Longest Day: Have your students keep track of sunrise and sunset times for a week or longer and use this to determine the number of hours of daylight each day. Have students take turns plotting this information on a

class graph to provide a visual display of the changes. For the most dramatic demonstration, have students begin plotting before December 21 (the shortest day) and continue into January.
2. Night Life: Have students work in small groups to find out more about these animals that are active at night: bats, fireflies, opossums, and owls.

Answers

1. Answers will vary but should go from bright oranges to mauves and charcoal grays; 2. Descriptions will vary but should include dark color, bright stars, and possibly the moon; 3. Answers will vary but should noticeably drop; 4. Should have become cooler because heating effect of sun is gone; 5. Answers will vary but should show distinct differences caused by different animals being active and even distinctly different city noises.

Resources

Sun Fun by Caroline Arnold. New York: Franklin Watts, 1981.
Sun and Light by Neil Ardley. New York: Franklin Watts, 1983.

Plane Tactics
(pp. 44–45)

Supplies

A copy of the worksheet for each child. To complete this activity, each student will also need a plastic straw, scissors, tape, and a measuring tape or yardstick.

Background Information

There are three main parts to an experiment: the manipulated variable, the responding variable, and the controlled variables. The manipulated variable is whatever is changed in the experiment. The responding variable is the particular result that is being watched or measured. And the controlled variables are any factors or conditions other than the one being manipulated that are kept from changing so they won't affect the results.

As students experiment, they need to plan to change the manipulated variable in a specific way. Then they need to compare the results caused by this change to what can normally be expected to happen. They also need to plan in advance what results they will be observing and pay very close attention to controlling anything else that could affect those results. This careful approach to experimentation will let your students be sure that any change that they observe was caused by the manipulated variable.

Finally, students need to plan to repeat any test they perform at least three times. Something which happens only once could be a freak occurrence.

Teaching Strategies

Establish a test-flight range down a long hall or outdoors if the weather, including the wind, can be counted on not to interfere. This will allow students to compare their data by having the same testing conditions. Set up the plane-building materials at a center. Have students work on this activity in small groups with each team member constructing and testing his or her own plane. Allow time for groups to share the changes they tested and which changes produced the best results. Have the groups continue experimenting by tackling the challenge presented in the On Target extender activity.

Extenders

1. On Target: Now challenge your students to work in small groups to design a straw plane that will accurately land on a given target, such as a medium-size to large circle of colored paper. Allow time for students to share what they discover as they tackle this problem-solving situation.

Answers

1. Answers will vary but should include changing position of paper loops, changing sizes of loops, changing length of straw, and weight of plane; 2. Students will undoubtedly think of additional variables to control, but the list should include position from which plane is launched, way in which plane is launched, wind speed, and wind direction; 3. Finding an average helps make up for differences in the way variables are controlled; 4. Answers will vary but should reflect logical thought.

Resources

The Paper Airplane Book by Seymour Simon. New York: Puffin, 1971.
Flying Paper Airplane Models by Frank Ross. New York: Lothrop, Lee & Shepard, 1975.
How to Have Fun Making Paper Airplanes by Creative Educational Society. Chicago: Children's Press, 1973.

Rings a Bell
(p. 46)

Supplies

A copy of the worksheet for each child. Each group will also need four identical glass quart jars, a measuring cup, water, and a metal spoon.

Background Information

Sounds are created when something vibrates. These vibrations move out in all directions from the vibrating source through a solid, a liquid, or a gas in waves. Different wave patterns produce very different sounds. A sound's pitch—how high or low the sound is—depends on the number of waves passing any given point each second. The more waves, the higher the pitch. Or, in other words, the faster something vibrates, the higher the pitch. The sound's amplitude— loudness—depends on the wave's size.

Teaching Strategies

This could be set up as a center activity or presented as a demonstration. Share the background information. Tell your students that they're looking for a pattern in order to make a prediction. Have one student strike the jars, following the pattern listed below to play a tune. Ask students to name that tune ("Mary Had a Little Lamb"). Use the extender activity to encourage innovative thinking as kids tackle the problem of producing sounds and finding ways to change sounds.
1,2,3,2–1,1,1
2,2,2–1,1,1
1,2,3,2–1,1,1
1,2,2,1,2,3

Extenders

1. Strike Up the Band: Challenge your students to create their own wind, string, and percussion instruments. To get them started, suggest blowing over pop bottles partly filled with water, plucking rubber bands stretched across an open box, and thumping on a

Using the Activities ....

large rubber sheet (formed by cutting open a rubber balloon) anchored over the top of a large-mouthed jar or cardboard carton.

Answers

1. Lower; because the pattern is the more water there is, the deeper the sound; 2. Answers will vary; Bonus Challenge: When you blow over the top, you're making the air vibrate and there is a tall column of air—the taller this column, the deeper the sound; When you strike the bottle, you're making the column of water vibrate. There is only a short column of water so a high tone is produced.

Resources

Sound And Music by Neil Ardley. New York: Franklin Watts, 1984.
Sound Experiments by Ray Broekel. Chicago: Children's Press, 1983.
The Magic of Sound by Larry Kettelkamp. New York: William Morrow and Company, 1982.

New and Improved
(p. 47)

Supplies

A copy of the worksheet for each child.

Teaching Strategies

The Imagine That! extender could be used as a motivational starter for this activity. Have students tackle this problem-solving activity in small groups to make them more comfortable being creative. Allow time for groups to share their improved products and present their commercials to the class.

Extenders

1. Imagine That!: Divide your class into small groups and give each group a common kitchen tool. Challenge your students to think of a way, other than the typical one, to use this tool.

2. Timely Solution: Tell your students to imagine that it is 1950 and there has been an accident. A truck loaded with liquid soap has crashed, spilling this slippery liquid all over the streets. Have your students work together in small groups deciding how to clean up the spill. The catch is that they can only use the technology that was available in 1950. Allow time for students to brainstorm and research their ideas, checking that any equipment or supplies they've chosen were available in the fifties. Then have the groups share their solutions.

Answers

1-4 Answers will vary but should show creativity and logical reasoning; Bonus Challenge: Should show creativity and clearly use one of strategies presented in Decoding Ads (p.7).

Resources

Be An Inventor by Barbara Taylor. San Diego: Harcourt Brace Jovanovich, 1987.
Great Discoveries And Inventions by David Lambert & Jane Insley. New York: Facts on File Publications, 1985.
Steven Caney's Invention Book by Steven Caney. New York: Workman Publishing Co., 1985.

A Little Bit Wild

Teachers' Notes ....

Getting Started

Kids are naturally fascinated by animals. The activities in this unit build on that high interest level, guiding students through thinking about animal groups and relationships, animals' basic survival needs, and special ways animals adapt for success in their environment. Students develop insights into habitats, including discovering that the environment around them is home to many different kinds of animals, even in a big city. They explore food chains. They use their observational skills to investigate animal behavior, and they creatively tackle real-life problems that are threatening wildlife today.

To start students investigating, arrange for an animal to visit your class. This animal doesn't need to become a permanent addition to your class unless you want it to. Parents, local veterinarians, or even pet shops can provide a visitor. Here are some hints for a successful visit.

1. Use a ten-gallon aquarium with a heavy wire-screen top for everything but the rabbits. The glass tank is easy to clean and generally escapeproof. It provides a clear view while preventing poking fingers. Definitely avoid the plastic Habitrails. These are difficult to clean, break easily, and soon become scratched and cloudy. For rabbits, the best cage is the commercially produced wire cage with a wire-mesh bottom and a tray that can easily be removed for cleaning.

2. Set up a cleaning schedule and have students help with this task. Spread cedar chips on the bottom of the aquarium cage. Then change these and scrub out the tank once a week. Put newspapers in the cage tray and change daily. Also, brush the bottom of the cage with an old hairbrush or steel wire bush and rinse the tray in chlorine bleach once a week.

3. Avoid exercise wheels. Animals may get a leg stuck and be injured. Empty toilet-paper tubes and shoe boxes with holes in them make the best toys for small animals.

4. Keep only one animal to avoid fights and unwanted offspring.

5. Feed animals the standard dry food available at pet stores; supply enough so that they always have some on hand. Guinea pigs also need special pellets containing a vitamin C supplement. Limit fresh food treats; too much will give the animals diarrhea. Remove any remaining fresh food after a day because it will spoil.

6. Keep the animal in a shady, cool spot.

Next, help your students be good hosts by introducing the animal to the children and demonstrating how the animal should be held and treated. If the animal will be visiting for more than a day or two, post a calendar and give each child a specific date to be the animal's keeper.

Allow time for students to interact with the animal and post the questions listed below near the animal's cage to direct their observations. Then take time to let the children share what they have discovered. And as the children work through this unit's activities, discuss whether this animal is a carnivore, an herbivore, or an omnivore, and call on them to consider its habitat requirements.

• What kind of food does it eat? What does the animal do as it eats?

• How does this animal play?

• Where does the animal usually sleep? How does the animal look when it's asleep?

Bulletin Board Ideas

1. Home Sweet Habitat: This interactive bulletin board should start students thinking about habitats. Start by dividing the bulletin board into habitats, such as ocean, jungle, desert, woodland, and freshwater pond. Include a paper pocket on each habitat, and in one corner of the board, attach a large paper envelope. Next, glue pictures of animals on three-by-five-inch index cards, number the backs of the cards, and tuck the cards inside the envelope. Then write directions for performing the bulletin board activity on the front of the envelope. Tell students to place each animal in the habitat where it would normally be found. And tell them to make a list of which card numbers were placed in each habitat. To make this activity self-checking, post a list of the correct card numbers for each habitat somewhere else in the room.

2. Sticky Puzzles: Make this bulletin board a puzzle that simulates how spiders use their silk to mark a trail. First, cover the board with colored paper. Attach four colored pictures (of anything interesting) out near the edges of the bulletin board. Next, cut four paper spiders out of four different colors of construction paper (or make each spider out of a colored pom-pom and attach eight pipe-cleaner legs) and attach these near the center of the board. Use a black marking pen to trace a wildly meandering path from one spider to one of the pictures.

Repeat, tracing a path for each of the other spiders to a different picture. Then post directions, challenging your students to find out where each spider went by tracing these "silk" trails with their fingers. Make this interactive bulletin board self-checking by posting the correct responses somewhere else in the room.

Name:_____

Let's Get Together.............

Directions: List at least five attributes (characteristics) that could be used to group these animals into two groups—those that have it and those that don't. You may want to check books and encyclopedias to find out information about the animals. Then use the attributes you picked to group the animals.

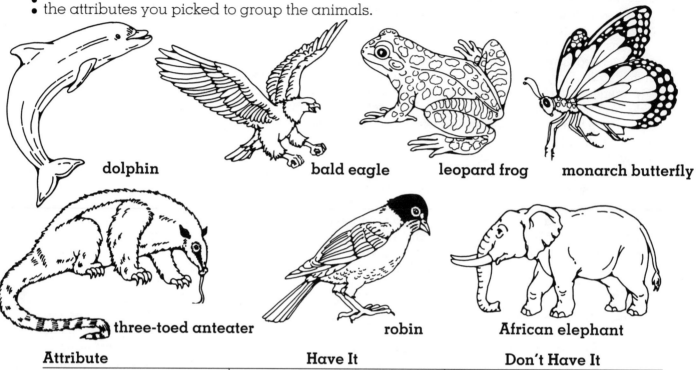

dolphin   bald eagle   leopard frog   monarch butterfly

three-toed anteater   robin   African elephant

Attribute	Have It	Don't Have It

Decide what attribute was used here to group the animals.

Have It	Don't Have It	Attribute
anteater, frog	elephant, butterfly eagle, robin, dolphin	_____

Oddballs..........................

Directions: Use books and encyclopedias to help you find out what each group of animals has in common. Circle the animal that doesn't belong in each group. Then tell why that animal is the oddball.

1.

frog   butterfly   praying mantis

_____
_____
_____

2.

_____
_____
_____

frog   cat   bird

3.

robin   penguin   ostrich

_____
_____
_____

4.

_____
_____
_____

deer   lion   cow

5.

kangaroo   elephant   rabbit

_____
_____
_____

6.

_____
_____
_____

kangaroo   sea horse   squirrel

Looking for a Home.............

Every animal needs food, water, shelter, and adequate space in which to live. The place that supplies these needs is called the animal's habitat.

Directions: Draw a line to connect each animal to the habitat in which it would normally live. Use encyclopedias and books to help you. Some of these animals may share a habitat.

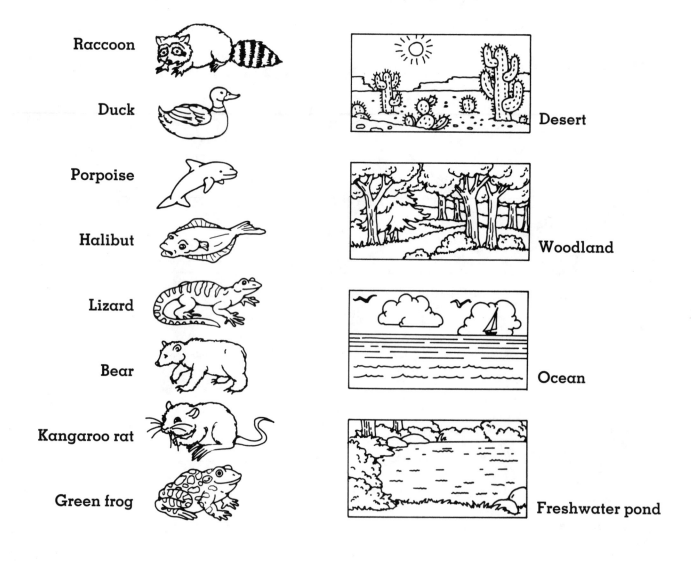

Raccoon

Duck

Porpoise

Halibut

Lizard

Bear

Kangaroo rat

Green frog

Desert

Woodland

Ocean

Freshwater pond

List what a polar bear needs from its habitat.

1. For food: _____

2. For shelter: _____

Mini Safaris...........................

Does wildlife live around your school?

Directions: Go outdoors and follow the steps below as you search for information about the wildlife living in your area. Then answer the questions.

1. Sit quietly for one minute. Listen carefully. List familiar sounds you hear. Tell what kind of animal you think made those sounds._____

_____

_____

2. Describe unfamiliar animal sounds you hear._____

_____

3. Continue to sit quietly for another minute. Look all around you. List any animals you see. If you don't know the animal's name, describe it._____

_____

_____

4. Look for signs that wildlife has been in this area, such as partly eaten leaves, tracks, a feather, or animal droppings. List them._____

_____

5. What kind of food does this habitat have to offer wildlife?_____

_____

6. Where might an animal find shelter in this habitat?_____

_____

Mystery Tracks..................

Directions: These tracks tell a story. First match the tracks to the pictures below to identify what animals were involved. Then decide what you think happened as you answer the questions below.

1. What animals were involved in the action? _____

_____

2. What do you think happened?_____

_____

_____

* Use the back of the page if you need more room.

3. Why did you come to that conclusion?_____

_____

Mouse   **Rabbit**   **Mountain Lion**   **Bird**

Name: _____

Fast Facts·····················

Directions: Analyze the graph to answer the questions about these speedy animals.

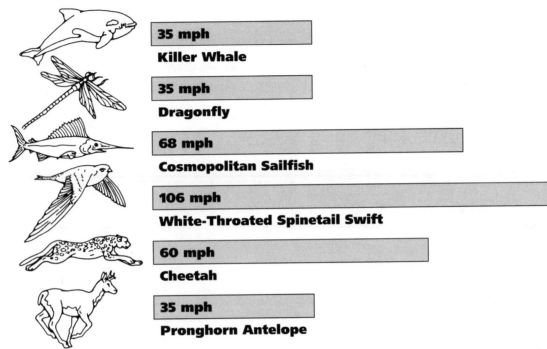

35 mph
Killer Whale

35 mph
Dragonfly

68 mph
Cosmopolitan Sailfish

106 mph
White-Throated Spinetail Swift

60 mph
Cheetah

35 mph
Pronghorn Antelope

1. Dragonflies are helpful because they eat a lot of mosquitoes, flies, and other insects.

How much faster than normal would a bug need to fly to escape a hungry dragonfly?

Most insects chug along at about five miles per hour. _____

2. Could a white-throated spinetail swift catch a dragonfly for lunch?_____

Why? _____

3. Why do you suppose a cheetah tries to sneak up on an antelope rather than simply

outrunning it?_____

_____

4. How many miles per hour faster is a cosmopolitan sailfish than a killer whale? _____

_____

Animal All-Stars...............

Directions: Use books and encyclopedias to find out which of the animals listed in the box at the bottom of the page deserves each award.

1. The largest animal in the world. The largest ever measured was 110 feet long and weighed 209 tons.

_____

2. The smallest mammal. It averages only 6 inches in length and usually weighs about 0.062 ounces.

_____

3. The world's champion jumper, this animal can leap 40 feet in one bound.

_____

4. No mammal can hold its breath as long—more than one hour.

_____

5. It's the slowest mammal on earth. Its average speed is only 6–8 feet per minute on the ground.

_____

6. When it comes to height, nobody comes close. It's as tall as 19 feet.

_____

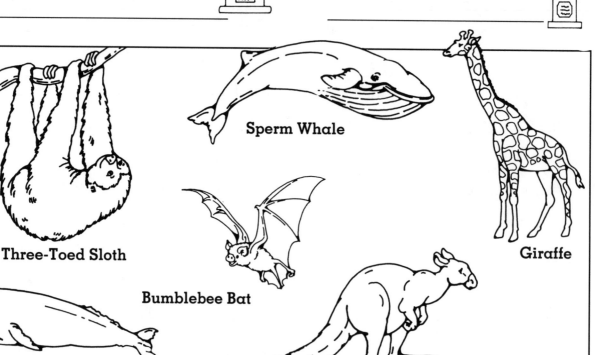

Three-Toed Sloth

Sperm Whale

Bumblebee Bat

Giraffe

Blue Whale

Red Kangaroo

Name: _____

What a Vore!.................................

Animals may be carnivores (meat eaters), herbivores (plant eaters), or omnivores (plant and meat eaters).

Directions: An animal's teeth are a good clue to what it eats. Examine the carnivore's, the herbivore's, and the omnivore's teeth shown below. Then answer the questions.

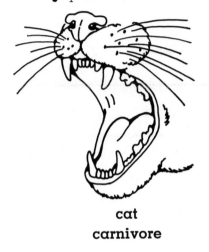

**cat
carnivore**

**cow
herbivore**

**human
omnivore**

1. How are the carnivore's teeth especially suited for eating meat? _____

_____

2. A cow uses its front teeth to snip off grasses. How do you suppose the cow uses its back

teeth? _____

_____

3. How can you tell that an omnivore eats both plants and meat?_____

_____

4. Look at this animal's teeth. Do you think it's a carnivore, an herbivore,

or an omnivore? Why?_____

_____

Let's Eat..

A food chain always begins with a green plant. Only green plants can produce their own food energy. In this food chain, the mouse eats the corn, the snake eats the mouse, then the hawk eats the snake. So the energy from the green plant is passed through the chain to the hawk. If the hawk dies and its body decays in the soil, it supplies minerals to help new green plants grow.

Directions: Cut out the pictures at the bottom of the page and paste them in the boxes to complete these food chains.

1. [ ], little fish, [ ], shark

2. duckweed, [ ], fish, [ ]

3. decaying leaves, earthworm, [ ]

plankton	tuna	water bug	robin	raccoon

Name: _____

Bird-Watchers' Club........

Directions: Follow the steps below to prepare this simple bird feeder. Then hang it outdoors and observe the birds that come to eat as you answer the questions.

- Collect a large pinecone, a piece of string ten inches long, one-quarter cup peanut butter, two tablespoons cornmeal, one-half cup birdseed, three slices stale bread, and one cup popcorn.

- Tie the string around the top of the pinecone. Spread peanut butter over the sides of the cone. Press the birdseed into the peanut butter.

- Hang the feeder outside on a branch or clothesline at a level you can reach easily. Tear the bread in pieces about the size of a dime or quarter. Scatter the bread crumbs and popcorn on the ground below your pinecone feeder.

- Check both feeders each evening, adding more food as needed.

1. Watch one bird eating at your hanging feeder. Draw a side view of its beak, showing the shape.

2. Describe this bird's behavior as it eats. _____

_____

3. Watch one bird eating at your ground feeder. Draw a side view of its beak, showing the shape.

4. In what way, if any, are this bird's eating habits different from the bird's at the hanging

feeder?_____

_____

Bird-Watchers' Club (Continued) · · · · · · · · · · · · · · · · · · ·

5. Do the birds usually eat alone or in groups at the hanging feeder?

_____ At the ground feeder?_____

6. Count how many birds you see eating at your feeders early in the morning, in the middle of the afternoon, and in the evening. Keep track of these diners for three days.

Feeder	Early Morning			Mid-Afternoon			Late Afternoon		
	Day 1	Day 2	Day 3	Day 1	Day 2	Day 3	Day 1	Day 2	Day 3
Hanging Feeder									
Ground Feeder									

7. What time of day did the most birds usually come to dine at the hanging feeder?

_____ At the ground feeder?_____

BONUS CHALLENGE ★★★★★★★

Birds have beaks that are specially designed for the kind of food they eat. Draw a line to connect each of these birds to its dinner.

hummingbird

hawk

cardinal

heron

woodpecker

nectar inside

Squirrel-Watching............

Directions: Observe one or more tree squirrels at home in the treetops as you answer the questions below.

1. How does the length of the squirrel's tail appear to compare to the rest of its body?

☐ Shorter   ☐ Same length   ☐ Longer

2. Watch for at least one minute. Describe everything you see the squirrel do with its tail.

3. Based on what you observed, circle each of the ways that you think a squirrel might use its big, bushy tail.

a. as a TV antenna   **b.** as a blanket   **c.** as a parachute

d. for balance   **e.** to hide under   **f.** to communicate

g. as a sunshade   **h.** as a rudder   **i.** as a towel

4. A squirrel is able to hang on, climb, and make long leaps because of its sharp claws, long tail, and excellent eyesight. Describe one squirrel's actions as it climbs or runs

along a branch. _____

_____

5. Notice the long whiskers. How do you suppose these help the squirrel? _____

_____

_____

Name: _____

Going Batty.............................

Directions: Use books and encyclopedias to help find the correct response to complete each of these facts about bats.

1. A bat's wings are made of
   A. feathers.
   B. living stretchy tissue.
   C. molded fat.

2. Flying foxes, the largest bats in the world, have about a six-foot wingspan and eat
   A. fruit and nectar.
   B. insects.
   C. human blood.

3. Many bats are very helpful because they feed on
   A. leaves.
   B. insects.
   C. human blood.

4. Bats do something most animals can't do. They
   A. are active mainly at night.
   B. have only one baby at a time.
   C. hang upside down for long periods.

BONUS CHALLENGE
★★★★★★★

Some bats send out very high-pitched whistles. From the echoes of these sounds bouncing back to them, they're able to piece together a "sound picture" of the world. This *echolocation* helps bats find food and fly without bumping into things in the dark. Pretend you are a bat and use echolocation to help you trace a path through the maze below.

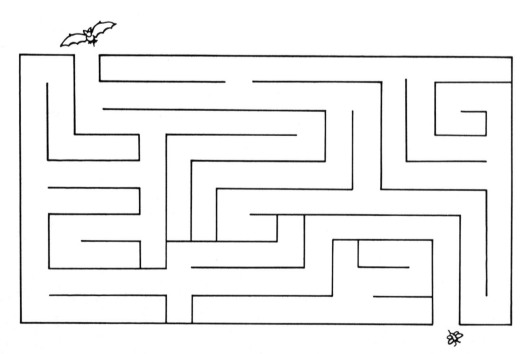

Skillful Spinners................

Directions: While they're probably most noted for the webs they build to trap food, spiders also find a lot of other uses for their silk. Perform the investigations below to explore some of these other uses.

A. Some spiders use their silk to travel. Shooting silk threads into the air, the spider is carried away by the wind. This mode of travel is called *ballooning.*

- Cut a strip of notebook paper ten inches long and two inches wide.

- Poke a small hole in one end of this strip; slip a paper clip through the hole.

- Next, hook the clip to the nylon line your teacher has set up. Be sure the clip will slide easily along the line. Then slide the strip to one end of the line and blow the strip toward the opposite end. Blow three times and measure along the floor below your model spider to see how far it traveled.

1. How far did your "spider" travel by ballooning? _____

_____

2. Why would this be a good way for spiders to travel? _____

_____

3. What could be one disadvantage of traveling this way?_____

_____

B. Spiders often wrap up uneaten food in silk.

- You'll need two identical slices of cheese and a piece of clear plastic wrap.

- Carefully wrap one slice of cheese in the plastic wrap. Place the two slices side by side on a paper towel on a table. Let sit overnight.

4. Which slice of cheese is drier?

☐ Wrapped ☐ Unwrapped

5. Compare both slices to a fresh slice. Which looks more like the fresh slice?

☐ Wrapped ☐ Unwrapped

Name: _____

For Sale......................................

Directions: Use books and encyclopedias to help find out which of the animals listed at the right would feel at home in each of these houses. Write the letter of that animal on the blank beside each house.

_____ **1.** This treetop house is called a drey. It has a twig floor about two feet across with walls and ceilings of woven leaves. The inside is lined with grass and soft bark strips.

A. Bald Eagle

_____ **2.** Called a lodge, this winter home is built of sticks and plenty of mud. It's located in a pond, but the inside is dry. Two underwater tunnels provide easy access to a nearby food supply of bark-covered branches.

B. Northern Fur Seal

_____ **3.** Special summer home available on the Pribilof Islands near Alaska. This flat, rocky beach front property provides an excellent view of the surrounding territories.

C. Gray Squirrel

_____ **4.** Lived in only one year, this home was custom-designed and built by the architect residents. Its walls, ceilings, and floors are entirely constructed of paper. Its numerous rooms are perfect for a large family.

D. Beaver

_____ **5.** This northern home's position high in the fork of a tree makes it a safe place for raising a family. It's completely open to the air, and its size—about three feet wide and five feet deep—makes it ideal for the larger couple. It's remodeled annually.

E. Bald-Faced Hornet

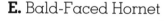

Name:_____

Partners...

Directions: Read about these animal partnerships. Then decide what benefits each partner gets from the relationship.

A rhinoceros is strong and powerful. And its horn, which is a hard-boned mass of hair, often more than four feet long, is a mighty weapon. A rhinoceros also has excellent hearing and a keen sense of smell. Its one weakness is that it can see only fifteen feet beyond its nose. The tickbird that rides on the rhinoceros's back can see very well, though. And whenever danger approaches, this little bird screeches and flaps its wings. At night, the tickbird roosts in a tree while the rhino goes off to eat. During the day, the tickbird strolls over the rhinoceros's hide, plucking off and eating any insects it finds.

1. How does the rhinoceros benefit from this partnership? _____

_____

2. How does the tickbird benefit? _____

_____

Some ants share a partnership with aphids that is similar to the one farmers share with a herd of dairy cows. The ants build special dirt homes to protect the aphids from rain. Each day, they carry the aphids to bushes where they suck plant juices. In return, the aphids secrete a sweet liquid when the ants stroke them. The ants eat this liquid.

3. How do the ants benefit from this partnership? _____

_____

4. How do the aphids benefit?_____

_____

 A person and a pet have a partnership. On the back of this page, describe how both the owner and the pet benefit from this relationship.

What Do You Think?..........

1. An area has been purchased, and developers want to clear away the forest to build new homes. An endangered species of birds nests in those trees every year, though. Some city residents want the development stopped to protect the birds. Do you think the housing plans should be allowed or blocked? Why?

_____

_____

_____

2. A number of animals, including alligators, have been hunted so heavily for their hide that they're in danger of becoming extinct. Suppose you really want a pair of alligator-skin boots. The label on the boots says the skins are from an alligator farm. Will you buy the boots? Why or why not?

_____

_____

_____

3. An insect pest is causing terrible crop damage. Farmers want to introduce a type of bird that eats this insect. That bird is native to Asia, though, and has no natural enemies here. Should the bird be introduced to stop the insect pest? Why or why not?

_____

_____

_____

Using The Activities

Let's Get Together
(p. 60)
Oddballs
(p. 61)

Supplies

A copy of each worksheet for each child. Students will also need access to encyclopedias and books about animals.

Background Information

An *attribute* is any special feature or trait, such as size or the ability to fly, that can be used to identify something. Attributes can be used to sort animals into two groups—those that have the attribute and those that don't. Officially, scientists use attributes to divide animals with similar characteristics into groups called *phyla*. These phyla include the platyhelminthes (flatworms such as planaria), annelida (segmented worms such as earthworms), arthropoda (animals such as crayfish and insects), mollusca (animals such as snails and oysters), echinodermata (starfish), and chordata (animals with backbones). The phylum chordata is further divided into classes, including mammalia (animals that are warm-blooded—meaning their body temperature remains about the same despite changes in the environmental temperature—have body hair, and usually nurse their young with milk produced by glands in the female's body).

Teaching Strategies

These activities help students practice their observational skills and creatively use what they observe to sort animals. If your students aren't already familiar with how to classify, introduce this skill before presenting these activities. First, have five children stand up, and give each child a large colored picture of an animal to display. Ask what special characteristics could be used to identify these animals. This list might include hair color, body size, ear shape, and the presence of a tail. Explain that such special features are called attributes. Then have your students use one attribute, such as large ears, to group the animals. Direct the chidren holding pictures of animals with large ears to move to one side of the room and those holding pictures of animals without large ears to move to the opposite side of the room. Repeat this process several times, allowing students to name an attribute and point out which animals belong in the group that has that attribute and which animals belong in the group that does not have that attribute.

Answers

Let's Get Together: While other attributes are likely, here is one set of possibilities: Ability to fly—eagle, robin, monarch butterfly / elephant, anteater, dolphin, green frog; Four legs—elephant, anteater, green frog / dolphin, eagle, robin, monarch butterfly; Have feathers—eagle, robin / elephant, anteater, monarch butterfly, green frog, dolphin; Lay eggs—eagle, robin, monarch butterfly, green frog / elephant, anteater, dolphin; Have beaks—eagle, robin / elephant, anteater, dolphin, monarch butterfly, green frog; Bonus Challenge: Catch food with tongue. **Oddballs:** 1. Praying mantis, because the others all change their form as they mature. A praying mantis hatches looking like an adult; 2. Cat, because it's the only one that doesn't lay eggs; 3. Robin, because it's the only one that flies; 4. Lion, because it's the only meat eater; 5. Elephant, because it doesn't jump; 6. Squirrel, because its young don't develop in a pouch.

Extenders

1. Animal Hunters Game: Have your students bring in pictures of animals. Trim pictures and mount them on five-by-seven-inch index cards. Create a deck of at least fifty of these cards. Two to four students can play. Each player is dealt five cards to start, and then one card is turned up to start a discard pile. Play moves to the right of the dealer. At the beginning of each turn, the player may take either one card from the deck or the entire discard pile. The player next lays down any group of animals, from a pair to a group of five, that have an attribute in common, announcing what that attribute is. The attribute must be logical and acceptable to the other players. The turn ends when the player discards one card. The game ends as soon as any person gets rid of all of his or her cards. The winner is the person who has collected the most animal cards sorted into groups.

2. Zookeeper: Have students pretend that they're in charge of a new zoo being built for your community. Explain that their job is to decide what animals should be grouped together to save money, to conserve space, and to make the best presentation for zoo visitors. You may want to let students tackle this problem in groups. Allow time for students to share their ideas. If possible, end with a trip to the zoo, paying special attention to what attributes were actually used to group the animals. (Also see Zoo Safari, pp. 98–99.)

...Using The Activities..............................

Resources

Amazing Facts About Animals by Gyles Brandreth. New York: Doubleday & Company, 1981.
The Book of Beasts by John May & Michael Marten. New York: Viking Penguin, 1983.
How Animals Live by Philip Steele. New York: Franklin Watts, 1985.

Looking for a Home
(p. 62)
Mini Safaris
(p. 63)

Supplies

A copy of each of the worksheets for each child. Students will also need access to encyclopedias and books about animals. To complete the Mini Safaris activity, students will need to explore outdoors.

Background Information

Animals have a basic set of requirements for survival. They need food, water, shelter, and adequate space. An environment that meets all of an animal's needs is called its habitat. An animal may also have certain special features that make it especially suited to a particular environment. The camel, for example, has thick eyebrows to shade its eyes from the bright desert sun, cushioned foot pads that act like snowshoes for walking on shifting desert sands, and the ability to withstand as much as a six-degree increase in body temperature without any ill effects. People feel sick if their temperature rises by as little as two degrees.

Teaching Strategies

Prepare your students for these activities by sharing the background information about habitats. Display pictures of different environments, such as oceans, jungles, freshwater ponds, woodlands, and deserts. Discuss together what each of these environments has to offer in the way of food, sources of water, shelter, and room to live. Have students find and bring in or draw and color pictures of familiar animals that are at home in each of the habitats you display. Use the Looking for a Home activity to provide practice relating wildlife to habitats. Then take the class outdoors and have students work in small groups to complete the Mini Safaris activity. Allow time for the groups to share what they discover and to draw class conclusions about the habitat provided by your community.

Answers

Looking for a Home: Freshwater pond—duck, green frog; Ocean—porpoise, halibut; Woodland—bear, raccoon; Desert—lizard, kangaroo rat; Bonus Challenge: A polar bear needs water, fish, and shelter from the wind and snow. **Mini Safaris:** 1–6. Answers will vary but should be logical responses for your area's environment.

Extender

1. Habitat Under Glass: Assign groups to work together to produce a mini habitat in a gallon glass jar or a five- to ten-gallon aquarium. Have students plan what the habitat will need to supply the needs of earthworms and/or insect life from your area. When this mini habitat is ready, allow time for the groups to collect wildlife and install it in its new home. Be sure the mini habitats have secure lids that allow air to enter but prevent residents from escaping. Have your students observe the wildlife's behavior up close for several days. Then have them release the animals.

Resources

How Animals Behave: A New Look at Wildlife by Editors. Washington, D.C.: National Geographic Society, 1984.
How Animals Live by Philip Steele. New York: Franklin Watts, 1985.

Mystery Tracks
(p. 64)

Supplies

A copy of the worksheet for each child.

Background Information

An animal's feet are specially adapted to help it survive in its habitat. Here are a few examples: Camels have thick, cushioned soles to protect them from burning heat and two wide toes that spread to keep them from sinking into the shifting sand.

Houseflies have a hairy pad coated with a gluelike substance on their feet. This lets them walk upside down on the ceiling. Flies can also taste with their feet. (If people could do that, they'd watch more carefully where they step.)

Mountain goats have curved hooves. This gives them suction-cup action as they dart along narrow mountain ledges.

A cat's toes have elastic muscles to retract their claws for nearly silent walking.

Woodpeckers have two toes pointed forward and two aimed backward for perfect balance while pecking at bugs on the side of a tree.

People often imitate an animal's specialized feet as they outfit themselves for various activities. For example, flippers improve a swimmer's

Using The Activities ....

performance, and cleated shoes keep football players and mountain climbers from slipping.

Teaching Strategies

Before performing these activities, divide the class into two teams and hold a thumbless relay to give your students a feel for what it's like to have a paw. Compile a class list of other animals with special feet. These could include the kangaroo (hopping), the horse (hooves to withstand pounding pressure), and the woodpecker (forward- and backward-pointing toes to brace itself on the side of a tree). Use the Mystery Tracks activity to encourage students to use their observational skills and make inferences to creatively tackle problem solving.

Answers

Mystery Tracks: 1. Rabbit, bird, mouse, bobcat; 2. Answers will vary but one possible solution is that the rabbit, mouse, and bird came to eat something at that spot, possibly at different times. The bird flew away, the mouse ran away, and the bobcat caught the rabbit, ate it, and then left; 3. Answers will vary but should present logical inferences based on observations of the tracks.

Extenders

1. Step On It: Spread a long strip of butcher paper on plastic or newspapers. Have student volunteers dip their bare feet in tempera paint and step onto a sheet of plain white paper to make one set of footprints. Then have them walk down the long sheet of paper. Have someone hold on to the student volunteers' hands as they make these prints to be sure they don't slip. Provide a plastic wading pool full of water and plenty of paper towels

at the end of the paper strip for students to clean their feet. Write the name of each student volunteer on the single sheet with their footprints. Tape the long strip of prints to the wall and display the individual prints around it. Number the footprint trails on the long strip and challenge your students to identify who made each trail. You may also want students to measure and compare footprint lengths or stride lengths (distance between one set of right and left footprints).

2. Foot Work: Have your students draw or find pictures of different kinds of special footwear that people wear to help them do different jobs. For example, snowshoes, skis, flippers, cleats, ice skates, tap shoes, and ballet slippers.

3. More Mystery Tracks: Challenge your students to make up their own track stories in three parts. Then have the students exchange and try to track down the solution to these mysteries. You could have students draw their own tracks, carve potatoes cut in half to create track stamps, or send for rubber animal-track stamps. Stamps of a variety of real animals are available inexpensively through Outdoor Products and Programs, P.O. Box 1492, Oxford, Mississippi 38566.

Resources

Crinkleroot's Book of Animal Tracks and Wildlife Signs by Jim Arnosky. New York: Putnam Publishing Group, 1979.
Exploring Winter by Sandra Markle. New York: Atheneum, 1984.
Let's Look at Tracks by Ann Kirn. New York: Putnam Publishing Group, 1969.

Fast Facts
(p. 65)
Animal All-Stars
(p. 66)

Supplies

A copy of each of the worksheets for each child.

Background Information

Speed can make the difference between catching food and going hungry. Or from another point of view, speed can make the difference between eating lunch and being eaten for lunch.

The killer whale is part of a fast pack of ocean hunters. Often traveling in groups of forty or more, these marine mammals chase down seals, walruses, dolphins, and even giant whales. A killer whale pursuing its prey may reach speeds of up to thirty-five miles per hour.

While most snakes depend on stealth and ambush their prey, the black mamba wriggles off in hot pursuit. Clocked as the fastest land snake, it holds a record for being able to travel about seven miles per hour across flat land or through trees. This snake holds another record; it can strike with deadly swiftness across a distance equal to nearly forty percent of its body length—about five feet. Now that's grabbing a quick bite!

The cheetah is the fastest short-distance runner, averaging speeds of up to sixty miles per hour for about 200 yards. The pronghorn antelope is the long-distance land champ; it can reach speeds of fifty-five miles per hour for short sprints and then keep going at about thirty-five miles per hour for as many as four miles.

In an effort to survive, animals hold other records. The red kangaroo, for example, can jump more than forty feet in a single leap. A cougar can't jump quite as far (only about thirty feet) but it can leap as much as eighteen feet into the air. That's a record. The blue whale holds the record just for being the biggest. This mammal may grow to more than 100 feet in length and weigh more than 150 tons. The giraffe is the tallest land mammal, with a body that stretches as high as nineteen feet.

Teaching Strategies

Use both of these activities to help students discover interesting facts about animals. Help your students draw the conclusion that the animal record holders are better able to survive because of these special abilities. Use the Fast Facts activity to provide students with an opportunity to analyze a graph to collect information.

Answers

Fast Facts: 1. More than thirty-one miles per hour faster—thirty miles per hour would make it even with the dragonfly and it needs to travel even faster to escape; 2. Yes, it flies much faster; 3. To increase its chances for catching its prey; 4. It's thirty-three miles per hour faster.
Animal All-Stars: 1. Blue Whale; 2. Bumblebee Bat; 3. Red Kangaroo; 4. Sperm Whale; 5. Three-Toed Sloth; 6. Giraffe.

Extender

Going for the Record: Challenge your students to compete against the animal champions. Have each student figure out how many bumblebee bats it would take to equal their weight, how many of themselves placed foot to head would be needed to be as tall as a giraffe.
Have them compare how far they can jump with the red kangaroo's record and how slowly they can move in one minute compared to the three-toed sloth's pace. Go outdoors to mark off the length of a blue whale. Your students may want to lie down head to toe to see how many of them it would take to equal this giant's length.

Resources

Animal Superstars: Biggest, Strongest, Fastest, Smartest by Russell Freedman. Englewood Cliffs, New Jersey: Prentice-Hall, 1984.
How Speedy Is a Cheetah? Fascinating Facts About Animals by Edward Knapp. New York: Putnam Publishing Group, 1986.
The Biggest, Smallest, Fastest, Tallest Things You've Ever Heard Of by Robert Lopshire. New York: Crowell Junior Books, 1980.

What a Vore!
(p. 67)
Let's Eat
(p. 68)

Supplies

A copy of each of the worksheets for each child. To perform the Let's Eat activity, students will also need scissors and glue.

Background Information

An animal's teeth are especially suited to the kind of food it eats. And likewise, by examining an animal's teeth, you can get a good idea of what kind of food it eats. Animals are generally divided into three eating groups—carnivores, herbivores, and omnivores.

A carnivore is a meat eater, and its teeth usually also have to help kill the food. These teeth are sharp and pointed for tearing meat and crunching bones. Back molars are designed to chew.

An herbivore is a plant eater. Because plants are tough and wear down teeth, many herbivores have teeth, specially designed for snipping off plants, that slowly wear away with use but never stop growing. Special chewing teeth are flat with hard ridges to grind up the plant material.

An omnivore eats both plants and meat. So its teeth are a mixture of sharp points for biting and low, flat teeth for grinding.

A food chain passes food energy on from animal to animal. Every food chain begins with a green plant because only green plants are able to produce their own food. This food-making process is called *photosynthesis*. Plant-eating animals eat the green plants, and then meat eaters eat the plant eaters. Usually in a food chain, smaller animals are eaten by larger animals. This chain becomes a cycle when the meat eater dies and its body decomposes, returning minerals to the soil, which helps green plants grow.

Teaching Strategies

Use the What a Vore! activity to introduce students to the terms *carnivore*, *herbivore*, and *omnivore*. Have them examine their own teeth in a mirror to determine which ones help them eat meat and which ones help them eat plants.

Introduce the activity Let's Eat by explaining a food chain as described in the background information. As a class, develop food chains for which people are the final consumers. For example, cows eat green plants, and people eat beef.

Answers

What a Vore!: 1. Pointed, sharp teeth for biting and tearing and back teeth designed for cutting and chewing; 2. These flat teeth are just right for grinding the plants it eats; 3. There are both sharp, pointed teeth, for tearing and cutting, and flat teeth, for grinding; 4. Carnivore, because all the teeth are sharp and pointed. **Let's Eat:** 1. plankton, tuna; 2. water bug, raccoon; 3. robin.

Extenders

1. Food Chains: Have your students work in groups to create food chains. Give each group strips of paper that are two inches wide and six inches long. Some of these strips should be green. Have students write one segment of their food chain on each strip, starting with a green plant on a green strip. Then have them make these strips into loops—gluing or stapling them together—to form a chain. Have your students try to make chains for an ocean habitat, a forest habitat, a desert habitat, and so on.

2. Bite on It: Have a dentist or oral hygienist visit your class to share information about proper dental care. Have an orthodontist visit to discuss the importance of well-positioned teeth and having a well-structured bite. Have students prepare for these visits by writing questions they would like to ask the experts. Select which questions students will ask.

Resources

What Big Teeth You Have! by Patricia Lauber. New York: Crowell Junior Books, 1986.
How Animals Behave: A New Look at Wildlife by Editors. Washington, D.C.: National Geographic Society, 1984.

Bird-Watchers' Club
(pp. 69–70)

Supplies

A copy of the worksheet for each student. To complete this activity, each student will also need a large pinecone, a piece of string ten inches long, one-quarter cup peanut butter, two tablespoons cornmeal, one-half cup bird seed, three slices of stale bread, and one cup popcorn. You'll want to spread out sheets of waxed paper or provide paper plates for the children to work on while preparing their pinecone feeders. If this is to take home, they'll also need two self-sealing plastic bags—one to carry the pinecone feeder and one for the ground-feeder materials.

Background Information

Putting out bird feeders is a great way to lure birds close enough to easily observe feeding behavior. A bird's beak is usually a good clue to what it eats. For example, a warbler has a thin, pointed beak to pick bugs from leaves. A hawk has a sharp, curved beak for tearing meat. A hummingbird's beak is like a long straw for sipping nectar from flowers. A finch has a fat, pointed beak to break open seeds. Different birds also prefer to eat at different levels. For example, sparrows, towhees, juncos, and finches prefer eating off the ground. Woodpeckers, nuthatches, and chickadees, however, prefer their food suspended above the ground. Books about birds can help interested students identify the specific birds that are visiting their feeders.

Although scientists and enthusiastic amateurs watch for birds year-round, every year on Christmas Day thousands of people participate in an organized bird count. The Christmas Day count was started in 1900 by Frank M. Chapman, who was then the chairman of the Bird Department of the American Museum of Natural History in New York City and was one of the founders of the National Audubon Society. For more information on participating in this annual census, write to the National Audubon Society, 950 Third Avenue, New York, New York 10022.

Teaching Strategies

This activity is designed to encourage students to make careful observations of animals and their behavior, just as a scientist would. Students are also encouraged to appreciate the wildlife with which they share their environment.

Have students perform this as a take-home activity, or set up the feeders at a spot where students can observe them at school—perhaps through a classroom window. Allow time for students to observe and then have them share what they discover. You may want to have students compile their bird counts on a class chart and compute an average.

Answers

1. Answers will vary but should show a bird with a short, pointed beak typical of seed eaters; 2. Answers will vary but should provide a detailed description of a bird eating at this feeder; 3. Answers will vary but should also show a short, pointed beak because this is also a seed eater; 4. Answers will vary but should describe ground behavior, such as walking around before eating; 5. Answers will vary, but birds are more likely to feed

individually at the hanging feeder and in groups at the ground feeder simply because of the space allowed; 6. Answers will vary; 7. Answers will vary depending on the birds that visit the feeders; Bonus Challenge: hummingbird/flower nectar; hawk/mouse; cardinal/seeds; heron/fish; woodpecker/insects in bark.

Extenders

1. Guess Who's Coming to Dinner: Encourage your students to use bird books to help them identify the birds that are eating at their feeders. Ask students to bring in pictures of birds, then label them, and display them to help students identify different birds.

2. Build Birdhouses: Obtain directions for easy-to-build birdhouses. (Plans for building a bluebird house are available from The North American Bluebird Society, Inc., P.O. Box 6295, Silver Spring, Maryland 20906.) Supply materials for these and set up a center for birdhouse building. If possible, arrange for parent volunteers to visit and help students construct simple birdhouses.

Resources

A Bird Watcher's Handbook by Laura O'Biso Socha. New York: Dodd, Mead & Company, 1987. *The Bird Watcher's Bible* by George Laycock. New York: Doubleday and Company, 1976. *Invite a Bird to Dinner* by Beverly Courtney Crook. New York: Lothrop, Lee & Shepard, 1978.

Squirrel-Watching
(p. 71)

Supplies

A copy of the worksheet for each child. Students will need a place to observe squirrels in action and time to observe them.

Background Information

There are three kinds of squirrels—ground squirrels, tree squirrels, and flying squirrels. Ground squirrels live in burrows. They're active during the day, and they hibernate during the long, cold winter months. Tree squirrels and flying squirrels live in the treetops. Tree squirrels are active during the day, and flying squirrels are active at night. Although these two kinds of squirrels may sleep inside a shelter during bad weather, they don't hibernate.

A tree squirrel prefers to live in a hole in a tree, but if one isn't available, it will prepare a leaf nest called a *drey*. Tree squirrels are omnivorous—eating nuts, seeds, fruit, insects, and birds' eggs. They eat about two pounds of food a week. They often bury nuts to store them for later. Their side-placed eyes give them a wide range of vision as they watch out for their enemies: owls, hawks, buzzards, dogs, foxes, and cats.

A tree squirrel has many uses for its big, bushy tail. It's a sunshade on a hot day, a blanket when it's cold, a parachute if it falls, a balance when it's running, a rudder when it changes direction suddenly, and, above all, a means of communicating.

Teaching Strategies

Like the Bird-Watchers' Club, this activity encourages students to use their observational skills the way a scientist would to collect information about animal behavior. Make this a take-home activity. Allow time for students to share what they discover.

Answers

1. Same length; 2. Answers will vary but should provide a detailed description of tail movements; 3. b, c, d, e, f, g, h; 4. Answers will vary but should provide a detailed description of the squirrel's movement, including how it uses its tail as a balance and a rudder during quick direction changes; 5. The whiskers provide a warning system. They stick out just as far as the biggest part of the squirrel's body and help it know if it has enough room to get through when it sticks its head in a hole.

Extenders

1. Squirrel Census: Visit a park. Have your students each take an area, counting the squirrels they spot. Combine these counts to determine the total number of squirrels observed. Discuss what natural features probably make this park a good squirrel habitat.

2. A Squirrel's Life: Say to your students, "What if you could be a squirrel?" Ask them what they would like about being a squirrel and what they would dislike about it.

Have them write a first-person story about being a squirrel, using what they've learned about squirrels by observing them.

3. Squirrel Talk: Squirrels use their tails as well as their voices to communicate. After having observed the squirrels, have your students tell what tail motions they think these animals use to express anger, joy, and fear.

Resources

Grey Squirrel by Editors of Oxford Scientific Films. New York: G. P. Putnam's Sons, 1982. *Tree Squirrel* by Colleen Stanley Bare. New York: Dodd, Mead &

Using The Activities

Company, 1983.
We Watch Squirrels by Ada and Frank Graham. New York: Dodd, Mead & Company, 1985.

Going Batty
(p. 72)

Supplies

A copy of the worksheet for each student. Students will also need access to encyclopedias and books about animals.

Background Information

There are nearly 1,000 different kinds of bats. The largest bats, the flying foxes of Australia and southeast Asia, have wingspans as big as six feet across. The smallest, the bumblebee bat, is only about as big as a jelly bean. Bats are the only flying mammals. Unlike most other animals, they are able to hang upside down for long periods of time. Different kinds of bats eat different kinds of food. Many are insect eaters. Some eat nectar, and vampire bats eat blood.

Bats often live in colonies. Really large colonies may consist of many millions of bats. Bats usually reside in caves, coming out at night to hunt for food. To fly without running into obstacles and locate food in the dark, many bats emit high-pitched squeaks and then listen to the returning echoes.

In the winter, some species of bats hibernate. Others migrate long distances to escape the cold weather.

Teaching Strategies

To introduce this activity, bounce a ball off a wall and catch it. Explain that this is what happens with the high-pitched sounds that bats emit. And that by interpreting these echoes, bats

are able to piece together a "sound picture" of the world around them. This process of using sounds to see is called *echolocation*. Allow time for students to complete the activity. As you discuss the correct responses, lead students to the conclusion that bats are not the monsters of the night that they are often portrayed as in movies.

Answers

1. B; 2. A; 3. B; 4. C; Bonus Challenge:

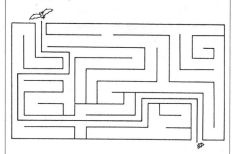

Extenders

1. Bats Did It First: Have your students find out more about sonar, an echolocation system that people use to see obstacles deep under water.

2. Sound Direction: While people don't use echolocation, they often use sound clues to detect direction. Have students work as partners. While one person sits with his or her eyes closed, have the partner snap his or her fingers at a specific compass point (N, NE, E, SE, S, SW, W, NW). The listener should then announce what the direction was. Have the partner mark the number of correct responses. You may also want students to explore whether or not this listening skill improves with practice.

Resources

Bats by Alice Hopf. New York: Dodd, Mead & Company, 1985.
Bats by Sylvia Johnson. Minneapolis, Minnesota: Lerner Publications, 1985.
Bats in the Dark by John Kaufmann. New York: Crowell Junior Books, 1972.

Skillful Spinners
(p. 73)

Supplies

A copy of the worksheet for each student. Students will also need scissors, a sheet of notebook paper, a ruler, a paper clip, a nylon line stretched across the room, three identical slices of cheese (one kept refrigerated until the second day), and clear plastic wrap.

Background Information

A spider's silk is noted for its strength and elasticity. It's second only to fused quartz fibers and stronger than a steel strand of equal thickness. It can stretch to 100 times its original length before it breaks. The spider's silk is produced in the abdominal glands. To make the silk flow, the spider presses its *spinnerets*, special nozzlelike duct ends, against something and pulls away, drawing out strands. Each spinneret is like a sieve plate full of holes. So what appears to be only one thread of silk is actually hundreds of silk strands pressed together. The manufacturers of polyester and other man-made fibers have copied the spider's production method.

Spiders are most famous for spinning webs to trap food, but they use their silk in a lot of other ways. A spider may spin a single line to climb up or glide down. Young spiders often shoot silk threads into the air and ride away as these lines are blown by the wind. This method of travel is called *ballooning*. Spiders also mark their trails with silk so they never get lost. And spiders that want to stay home are likely to create a nest or burrow lined with silk.

Spiders also use silk to tie down struggling prey and store food—much like tucking leftovers into a plastic bag. Many female spiders also wrap their eggs in a protective silk cocoon.

Teaching Strategies

Prepare for this activity by stretching a nylon line (monofilament fishing line works well) across the room at a height your students can easily reach. Introduce this activity by sharing the background information about how spiders produce silk and the many different ways they use their silk. Put up a class bar graph and have each student record how far his or her "spider" traveled by ballooning. Before they perform this activity, discuss together some of the factors that could have affected how far the spider traveled. While your students will undoubtedly think of additional possibilities, this list should include how hard the student blows, the way the air is aimed at the spider, how close the blower is to the spider, and any other air currents in the room. Encourage your students to measure carefully.

Answers

1. Answers will vary; 2. It would provide a way to travel long-distance much faster and probably more safely than by walking; 3. They wouldn't know what dangers might be awaiting

them when they land; 4. Unwrapped; 5. Wrapped.

Extenders

1. Stories in Silk: *Charlotte's Web* by E. B. White is a famous story about a very clever orb-web-weaving spider that saves Wilbur the pig from becoming just another plate of pork chops. Read *Charlotte's Web*. Then have your students write their own story about how an orb-web-weaving spider saves the day.

2. It's a Spider's Life: Have your students select one of these spiders to investigate: black widow, tarantula, orb-web-weaving garden spider, trap-door spider, wolf spider, crab spider. Then have them write a story based on fact about one day in that spider's life.

Resources

Master Builders of the Animal World by David Hancocks. New York: Harper & Row, 1973.
Spiders by Illa Podendorf. Chicago: Children's Press, 1982.
Spiders by Jane Dallinger. Minneapolis, Minnesota: Lerner Publications Company, 1981.

For Sale
(p. 74)

Supplies

A copy of the worksheet for each child. Students will also need access to encyclopedias and books about animals.

Background Information

Not all animals build homes. Some stay on the move. And even some that build elaborate homes may be temporary residents, staying only long enough to raise their young.

The Northern fur seal wanders alone or in small groups all

winter. Then in May, the bulls (males) begin arriving on the Pribilof Islands near Alaska. They fight each other for a territory on this rocky land. Then the cows (females) are herded into harems by the bulls when they arrive a few weeks later. The pups are born in June or July, and the herd remains at this rookery for the next four months, allowing the young seals time to grow enough to face a winter in the open sea.

The bald-faced hornet queen builds a paper house. To produce the paper, she scrapes off thin slices of wood with her sharp, toothlike mouth parts and mixes them with saliva. Each room is a perfect six-sided cell. The queen builds only enough rooms to raise her first brood of workers. Later, as the workers take over the construction job, the hornets' paper house may grow as big as a basketball.

Beavers build lodges to provide their families with a winter shelter. Lodges are made of sticks cemented together with plenty of mud. The lodge is built in the water, but its floor is above water. Snug inside, the beaver family keeps warm by sharing body heat.

Squirrels prefer to live in a hole in a tree, but there are seldom enough holes to go around. So a squirrel builds itself a leaf nest, called a *drey*. To construct a drey, the squirrel first makes a platform of twigs about two feet across. Then it pokes together leaves and twigs to form what looks like a leafy pile. Winter leaf nests are built tight enough to be water- and windproof. Summer nests are made with air spaces for ventilation. The inside is lined with soft bark strips.

American bald eagles build

nests that they repair and reuse year after year when they return to their summer homes to lay eggs and raise their young. These nests, usually located in the fork of a large tree, are cone-shaped. They may be up to nine feet across, fill the tree fork twenty feet deep, and weigh as much as a ton.

Teaching Strategies

Allow time for students to work on this activity in small groups. Have each group choose one animal home to research, finding out more about it. The group could also find a picture of this home. Go over the answers together, allowing time for each group to present what they discover.

Answers

1. C; 2. D; 3. B; 4. E; 5. A.

Extender

More Animal Real Estate: Have student groups choose one of these animals' homes to investigate: ant, bee, prairie dog, orb-web spider, mole, and bat. Then have them write a real-estate-style advertisement for that home to share with the class.

Resources

Animal Architects edited by Donald J. Crump. Washington D.C.: National Geographic Books, 1987.
Animal Homes by Illa Podendorf. Chicago: Children's Press, 1982.
Exploring Summer by Sandra Markle. New York: Atheneum, 1987.

Partners
(p. 75)

Supplies

A copy of the worksheet for each child. Students will also need access to encyclopedias and books about animals.

Background Information

Animals are partners when both animals benefit from the relationship. The rhinoceros and the tickbird, for example, are such good partners that they can't live without each other. The rhinoceros, despite being big and powerful, has poor eyesight and can't see more than fifteen feet beyond its nose. So if the wind was blowing an enemy's scent away, and the enemy was quiet, the rhinoceros would be in big trouble.

Fortunately, the tickbird that rides on its back has excellent eyesight and screeches loudly at the first sign of danger.

If this doesn't get the rhinoceros's attention, the little bird will even peck its big partner on the head. The tickbird also benefits from this relationship by being able to eat the ticks that stick to the rhinoceros's hide. This keeps the bird well fed and the rhinoceros healthy. The tickbird also pulls out the rhinoceros's tough hairs to weave its nest.

Ants and aphids share a relationship that's similar to a farmer with a herd of dairy cattle. The ants build special dirt homes for the aphids and daily carry them to bushes where they can suck the plant juices. The ants also tend the aphids' eggs, helping them raise their young. In return, the aphids secrete a sweet liquid whenever the ants stroke them, and this is an important food for the ants.

Teaching Strategies

Do this as a class activity, reading the information aloud—sharing additional facts from the background information—and compiling a class list of answers. Then perform the extender activity to allow your students to experience working with a partner to accomplish a task.

Answers

1. He's warned of approaching danger and has ticks picked off his skin, which helps keep him healthy; 2. The tickbird gets a ready food supply of ticks and a supply of tough hairs with which to build its nest; 3. Ants are supplied with a sweet liquid food; 4. Aphids receive protection, shelter, and access to food; Bonus Challenge: The person receives companionship and sometimes protection or assistance. The pet receives protection, shelter, and food.

Extender

Teamwork: Divide students into partner groups. Have the partners sit back to back. Use an overhead projector to show a simple line drawing to one of the partners. Then have that student give oral directions to his or her partner to duplicate this drawing. Have these students check how closely their drawing duplicates the projected image. Discuss together what was difficult about giving these oral directions and how the directions could have been communicated more effectively.

Resources

How Animals Live Together by Millicent E. Selsam. New York: William Morrow and Company, 1979.
Natural Partnerships: The Story of Symbiosis by Dorothy Shuttlesworth. New York: Doubleday & Company, 1969.

Symbiosis: A Book of Unusual Friendships by Jose Aruego. New York: Charles Scribner's Sons, 1970.

What Do You Think?
(p. 76)

Supplies

A copy of the worksheet for each student.

Background Information

Loss of a habitat is one of the main reasons animal species have become endangered. Some animals can live only in a certain habitat. If that habitat is dramatically changed or eliminated, that animal moves. If enough habitats, particularly sites where the animals raise their young, are eliminated, the animals become endangered or even extinct. This is what has happened to the southern bald eagle. These birds have very specific nesting requirements. They mate for life and return to the same nesting site year after year. If the tree containing their huge nest has been cut down or the area around it has been built up in a way that makes the site unsuitable for the birds, they're likely to build another nest in the same area.

However, if no other nesting tree is available in that area, the birds may not nest. In recent years, the number of nesting pairs has dwindled to such an extent that the southern bald eagle population has become dangerously small.

When an animal has no natural enemies, breeding may quickly swell the animal population to huge proportions. This is what happened when English starlings were brought to the United States to attack an insect pest. The birds did eat the insect pest, but soon there were so many birds that they ate the farmers' crops as well as the insects, becoming pests themselves. Sometimes an introduced species may begin attacking a native species, reducing that animal or plant to endangered levels. That is what has happened to the wombat. This Australian marsupial, which eats mainly termites, has fallen prey to an introduced species. Unregulated hunting has also reduced the populations of numerous species, such as the Queen Alexandra birdwing butterfly, the snow leopard, and the humpback whale, to endangered levels.

Teaching Strategies

Have students work on this activity in small groups. Then allow time for the groups to share their opinions. Discuss together the importance of wildlife conservation.

Answers

1. Answers will vary but should reflect thoughtful consideration of the endangered species; 2. Answers will vary but should indicate an understanding of the threat of poachers to endangered species valued for their skin or fur; 3. Answers will vary but should express the problem created by introducing a species into an environment where it has no natural enemies.

Extenders

1. Rare Finds: Assign student groups to find out more about the special features and habits of one of the following endangered species: panda, whooping crane, bald eagle, American alligator, polar bear, flying fox (bat), orchid, sperm whale, green sea turtle, African elephant, black rhinoceros, Grevy's zebra, vicuna, green pitcher plant, and snow leopard. Also have your students try to find out why the animal has become endangered. Allow time for the groups to share what they discover.

2. Adopt a Whale: The Whale Adoption Project (320 Gifford Street, Falmouth, Massachusetts 02540) provides resource materials to help students learn more about endangered whale species. For a nominal fee, the class could also select one whale currently being tracked and studied (based on photographs) to support. The class will receive regular updates of this whale's sightings in order to plot the whale's travels on a map. This further provides an overview of whale migration and an opportunity to become personally involved with efforts to understand and save an endangered species.

Resources

Endangered Animals by Dean Morris. Milwaukee, Wisconsin: Raintree Publishers, 1984.
Endangered Animals by Lynn M. Stone. Chicago: Children's Press, 1984.
Rare and Unusual Animals by Nina Leen. New York: Henry Holt & Company, 1981.

Mini-Field Trips

···Teachers' Notes···

Getting Started

Traditionally, taking a field trip has implied climbing aboard a bus and venturing forth to investigate new vistas. Fortunately, it's possible to explore with the same sense of adventure much closer to home base—even within your own classroom—and still have lots of opportunities for discovery.

To get things started, take your class on a texture hike. You may go indoors or outdoors. Tell your students that along the way you want them to find things that have each of these textures: rough, smooth, gritty, slick, prickly, soft, furry, and bumpy. Then prepare a special notebook to record finds by writing each of the textures on a separate page. Since this hike focuses on touch, allow time for students to stop and feel items while they hunt. Or go on a color hike. Begin by having your students spot everything they can that's green. Keep on walking, but after a few minutes change the color to yellow, then to brown, and so forth.

If you have plenty available, pass out magnifying glasses. Then let your students use them to turn a familiar environment into an intriguing new world. Have them begin by examining the fabric of their own clothing, their fingertips (print side), and a friend's hair. Next, have them go outdoors to view leaves, buds on trees or shrubs, a small insect, and dirt. Depending on the season and your locale, think of additional items for students to investigate. Allow time for students to share what they discover. Encourage them to describe how things look different when magnified.

The following programs provide excellent resource materials to assist you in planning and conducting field-trip activities.

Expedition Yellowstone (Division of Interpretation, National Park Service, P.O. Box 168, Yellowstone National Park, Wyoming 82190)

Project Wild (P.O. Box 18060, Boulder, Colorado 80308)

Project Learning Tree (1250 Connecticut Avenue NW, Washington, D.C. 20036)

Bulletin Board Ideas

1. Armchair Safaris: Display colorful pictures of each of these different habitats: jungle, desert, ocean, freshwater lake, and forest. Label these habitats and staple a pocket next to each. To make a pocket, you could use a large manila envelope or staple shut the edges of a file folder. Then include directions that challenge your students to find facts about each of these habitats. Tell them to write each fact they find on a separate three-by-five-inch index card along with their name and put it in the pocket next to the habitat it describes. Add one catch: no one can repeat a fact. This will keep everyone reading the new facts as they're added. To ensure that everyone's motivated to dig up facts about the habitats, you may want to offer a certificate, a ribbon, or a special privilege to the person who contributes the most facts by the end of a set time period.

2. Close to Home: This activity will make being in your classroom an adventure. First, turn your bulletin board into a map of the classroom. Label ten familiar landmarks, such as the pencil sharpener, as key exploration sites. Next to each of these, post instructions for investigating each site using a different sense. For example, you might direct your students to touch the window and describe what they feel.

Or you might tell them to close their eyes while standing next to the bookcase, listen for one minute, and then list everything they hear. They could even be directed to peer into the wastebasket and describe what they see.

Name:_____

Bark Hunters......................

Directions: Follow the steps below as you collect bark rubbings from six different kinds of trees. You'll be able to tell that the trees are different because each kind of tree's bark is unique, with its own special color and pattern.

To prepare a bark rubbing:

• Hold a piece of plain white typing paper flat against the bark with one hand.

• Rub a brown crayon over the paper in one direction only. Write the real color of the bark below your rubbing.

• Cut out a piece of each rubbing and glue one on each of the boxes below.
  On the line below each box, tell the bark's real color.

1. color_____   **2.** color_____   **3.** color_____

4. color_____   **5.** color_____   **6.** color_____

Next, list at least four attributes (special characteristics) that you could use to sort the tree barks you collected. Then sort the bark rubbings into those that have that attribute and those that don't. Write the number of each bark rubbing in the column where it belongs.

Attribute	Has It	Doesn't Have It

Name:_____

Tree's Company......................

Directions: Choose one tree. Then answer the questions as you get to know this special tree.

1. How big around is your tree's trunk? Measure at the fattest point. _____

_____

2. Make a bark rubbing following the directions for Bark Hunters and glue it in the box below. Tell the real color of the bark and describe any special features you see on the bark, such as cracks or holes.

3. How far out does the tree canopy (leafy branches) extend? Measure from the trunk out

until the end of the longest branch is over your head. _____

_____

4. The tree's roots stretch up to seven times farther than

the canopy. How far out do the roots extend?

Multiply the answer in No. 3 by 7. _____

_____

Tree's Company (Continued) . . . .

5. Carefully draw and color a picture of one of your tree's leaves. Be sure you draw a complete leaf. Some tree leaves are made up of more than one leaflet. You can tell where the leaf's stem begins by looking for a bud (a tiny bump from which a new leaf will grow) at what you think is the base.

leaf

6. On a sunny day, check the air temperature in the open and again in the shade under your tree. How much cooler is it in the shade? _____

7. Sit or stand quietly under your tree for two minutes. Listen and look carefully. Describe all the sounds you hear. _____

_____

List any animals or signs of animal life that you see. _____

_____

8. What do you like best about your tree? _____

_____

Name: _____

That's Attractive!··················

Directions: Collect a bar magnet. Then find each of the items below and hold the magnet close to it. Check whether or not the magnet attracts that item on the chart.

Item	Will Attract	Won't Attract
1. A plastic sandwich bag		
2. A rubber-soled shoe		
3. A leather belt		
4. A wooden pencil		
5. A steel paper clip		
6. A drinking glass		
7. An aluminum soft-drink can		
8. An iron nail		
9. A tree leaf		
10. A stainless-steel spoon		
11. A rubber tire		
12. A T-shirt		

BONUS CHALLENGE ★★★★★★★ Based on what you discovered, put an X next to each item you predict the magnet will attract. Then test each item and put an X next to the items the magnet actually does attract.

Item	Predict Attracts	Attracts
13. A metal fork		
14. A newspaper		
15. A metal doorknob		

Hot Spots..

Directions: On a warm, sunny day, use an indoor/outdoor thermometer to check the temperature at each of the places listed on the chart below. Wait five minutes at each location before recording the temperature to allow the thermometer time to adjust.

Location	Temperature
1. Just outside the school's front door	_____
2. Next to your desk	_____
3. In the library	_____
4. In the school parking lot	_____
5. Under the closest tree to your classroom window	_____
6. Twenty feet from the south wall of your school	_____

7. Where was it hottest? _____

8. Examine that location carefully. Why do you think this was the hottest spot? _____

_____

_____

Set in Concrete...................

Concrete is man-made rock that is highly valued as a building material because it is easy to make, cheap, fireproof, watertight, and strong.

Directions: Answer the questions as you watch the concrete being prepared and hardening. Then find at least five places where concrete has been used around your school or in your community.

1. Describe how the concrete mix looked before the water was added._____

_____

2. How did the concrete mix feel? _____

_____

3. Tell what the concrete mix looked like after water was added. _____

_____

4. How did the wet concrete feel? _____

5. In what ways did the concrete change as it dried?_____

_____

6. List at least five places where concrete has been used around the school or in the community. Next to each, tell why you think concrete was a good material to use for that building job.

_____

_____

_____

_____

_____

Soil Search.........................

Directions: Collect one cup of each of three different-looking soils in self-sealing plastic bags. You'll also need a magnifying glass, three clear plastic cups, three strips of blue litmus paper, three strips of pink litmus paper, paper tape, measuring spoons, and water. Follow the steps below to investigate these soils and record your observations on the chart. Then answer the questions on the next page.

• Observe each soil's color.

• Examine the soil with a magnifying glass. Do the particles look big or little? Do they have sharp or rounded edges?

• Pinch a little bit of soil between two fingers. Do the particles stick together or fall apart?

• Put one strip of blue litmus and one strip of pink litmus in the bottom of a cup. Add three heaping tablespoons of soil. Tape a label on the side of the cup to identify the soil. Add just enough water to soak through the soil to the litmus paper. Then look at the wet strips through the bottom of the cup. If the blue strip turns pink, the soil is acid. If the pink strip turns blue, the soil is basic. If neither strip changes color, the soil is neutral. Repeat for each of the other soil samples.

Soil Sample (tell where found)	Color	Texture (describe particles)	Acid/Base/Neutral
1.			
2.			
3.			

Soil Search (Continued) . . . .

4. Dark gray or black soils usually contain more minerals and are better for growing plants. Which, if any, of your soils were these colors? _____

5. Alfalfa plants need more water to grow than many plants. An acre of alfalfa needs more than a million gallons of water before it's ready to harvest. Which of the soils you tested do you think would do the best job of letting water quickly soak down to the alfalfa roots? _____ Why? _____

_____

6. Azaleas grow best in acid soil. Which, if any, of the soils you tested would be good for growing azaleas? _____

BONUS CHALLENGE ★★★★★★★

This puzzle contains the names of some of the many animals that dig into the soil for food or shelter. Find and circle all 13 of these animals. Look across and down.

```
E   A   R   T   H   W   O   R   M
S   O   W   B   U   G   V   E   O
O   E   S   O   U   S   I   P   L
M   I   L   L   I   P   E   D   E
A   D   U   L   W   I   B   F   G
N   M   G   A   B   D   C   O   O
T   B   A   D   G   E   R   X   P
S   N   A   I   L   R   D   E   H
C   E   N   T   I   P   E   D   E
C   H   I   P   M   U   N   K   R
```

Name: _____

Tombstone Geology...........

Directions: Visit a cemetery to perform the activities. Then answer the questions.

1. Look for tombstones that are made of speckled rock. Those tombstones are made of granite. List all the different colors of granite that you can find in the cemetery.

_____

_____

2. Find a granite tombstone that has only part of the stone polished. Compare the polished and unpolished rock. In what ways did polishing change the granite?

_____

_____

3. Windblown grit and rain cause weathering that gradually erodes the surface of the stones. Use the dates carved on the tombstones to locate three that were erected as close as possible to these years: 1900, 1940, 1980. On which stone is the inscription the least sharp? _____

On which stone do the outlines of any carvings look the most weathered? _____

_____

4. Weathering can also cause rocks to crack. This is especially true if you live where it becomes cold enough so that water that seeps into cracks expands as it freezes. Look for a cracked tombstone. What year was it erected? (Check the date on the inscription.)

_____

_____

Name: _____

Zoo Safari ....

Directions: Visit a zoo to track down the answers to the questions below.

1. Watch an elephant for one minute. List all the ways this animal uses its long trunk.

_____

_____

2. Find out what the elephant eats. Is it an herbivore (plant eater), a carnivore (meat eater), or an omnivore (a plant and meat eater)? _____

3. Look at a tiger. In the wild, this animal sneaks through tall grass until it's close enough to ambush its prey. How do you think the tiger's striped coat helps it be a successful hunter? _____

_____

4. Find at least one kind of animal that lives in a group. What kind of animal is it?

_____

Why do you think living in a group would help this animal survive in the wild?

_____

_____

5. Find one animal that is listed as an endangered species. What kind of animal is it?

_____

Why do you think it is in danger of becoming extinct?` _____

_____

6. How can zoos help endangered species like the one you observed? _____

_____

Name:_____

Zoo Safari (continued)••••••••••••••••••••••••••••••

7. Find one animal that has a baby. What kind of animal is it?_____

List all the ways that the baby is different from the adult. _____

_____

8. Track down a bear. What kind of bear is it?_____

Watch for one minute. Describe everything the bear does. _____

_____

_____

9. Find a hippopotamus. Observe it for at least a minute. Why do you suppose this

animal's eyes and nostrils project above its head?_____

_____

10. Locate a monkey with a long tail. What kind of monkey is it? _____

Watch until this animal moves from one place to another above the ground. Describe

how it uses its tail to help it move._____

_____

11. What animal do you think is the most interesting to watch at the zoo?_____

Why did you particularly enjoy this animal? _____

_____

12. If you could be one of the animals you saw at the zoo, which one would you like to

become?_____Why?_____

_____

_____

Name:_____

Wild and Woolly Plants.....

Weeds are any uncultivated—and usually unwanted—plants. They're also usually very hardy, and they often grow in unlikely places.

Directions: Hunt for weeds and answer the questions below.

1. Name at least three places where you found weeds growing. _____

_____

2. Find at least one plant growing in a sidewalk crack. Look closely. In what ways does this plant seem to have adapted to life in such an unfavorable spot? _____

_____

3. Find a weed in bloom. Tell why you think people haven't chosen to cultivate this plant for its flowers._____

_____

4. Why could weeds growing on a bare, vacant lot be good for the environment?_____

_____

5. Find one dry dandelion flower. Carefully, working over a paper towel, pull out the puffs, one by one, counting the seeds. How many seeds made up that one dandelion flower? _____Why does this weed need to produce so many seeds?

_____

BONUS CHALLENGE ★★★★★★★

If you find any burrs stuck in your pet's fur or clinging to your clothes, carefully pull them free. These are weed seeds. Try planting the seeds (several may be planted together) in a small pot full of soil. Sprinkle on a little water as needed to keep the soil moist but not wet. Cover with clear plastic wrap and set the pot in a warm spot. Observe for two weeks. Do any of the seeds sprout? If so, transfer the young plants to their own pot and continue to watch their development.

Name:_____

Ants at Work............................

: **Directions:** Troop off to the nearest open field to perform these investigations.

1. Track down some ants. How many legs do ants have?_____

2. Watch one ant for a minute. How do the ant's antennae help it find out about its

environment?_____

_____

3. Sprinkle a few grains of sugar four inches away from the ants. Time how long it takes

for the ants to discover this treat. _____

4. Observe one of the ants carrying away the sugar. How does it pick up the sugar?

_____

How much does it carry at one time? _____

5. Describe how this ant moves its sweet burden. _____

_____

_____

6. Place a toothpick across the ant's path. How does it solve this problem? _____

_____

7. Follow the ants as they carry the sugar to their home. Do the ants all follow the same

trail or does each take a different path?_____

8. Most ants live in tunnels underground. How do you suppose the mound around the

entrance helps protect the ants' home? _____

_____

Gone Buggy ....

Directions: Catch a caterpillar. Put it in a glass jar with plenty of the kind of leaves it was eating when you found it. Cover the top of the jar with plastic wrap and anchor it with a rubber band. Punch plenty of tiny holes in the plastic with a pin. Add new leaves as needed until the caterpillar spins a cocoon. Keep the cocoon in the jar until you see the adult emerge. Then let it go. What you've observed is almost a complete life cycle. The stage you missed is the one in which the adults mate and the females lay eggs, which hatch into new caterpillars.

Draw and color a picture of each of the stages of the insect's life cycle that you observed.

caterpillar **cocoon** **adult**

BONUS CHALLENGE ★★★★★★★

Circle all 12 of the bugs hidden in this puzzle. Search across, down, and diagonally.

```
D  C  O  C  K  R  O  A  C  H
R  M  O  S  Q  U  I  T  O  C
A  M  O  T  H  D  E  J  V  R
G  H  O  U  S  E  F  L  Y  I
O  C  I  C  A  D  A  S  U  C
N  L  A  D  Y  B  U  G  L  K
F  R  E  N  Y  W  A  S  P  E
L  B  E  E  T  L  E  C  M  T
Y  B  U  M  B  L  E  B  E  E
```

Name: _____

Mission in Space..................

Directions: You have recently joined the science research colony on an alien planet in a distant galaxy. Your job is to select one of the exploration routes your teacher, the mission leader, has prepared for you. Use a compass to determine what direction to travel and advance the number of steps listed for each leg of your trek. At the end of each leg, carry out the tests for that area. Then record your observations.

End of Leg 1: Check the air temperature. _____

Note how much of the sky is cloud-covered (all, most, part, clear). _____

_____

End of Leg 2: Describe any plant life you see. _____

_____

End of Leg 3: Look for animals or signs of animal life. Do you believe animal life is

present? Why? _____

_____

End of Leg 4: Describe the planet's surface in this area. _____

_____

_____

End of Leg 5: Listen carefully for one minute. Describe what you hear. _____

_____

_____

End of Leg 6: Stand where you are and turn around slowly. List all the colors you

can see. _____

_____

Your mission is complete. Return to base.

... Using the Activities ....

Bark Hunters
(p. 89)
Tree's Company
(pp. 90–91)

Supplies

A copy of each of the worksheets for each child. To complete the Bark Hunters activity, students will need six sheets of plain white typing paper, a dark-colored crayon, scissors, and glue. To perform the Tree's Company activity, students will need a measuring tape, a sheet of plain white typing paper, a dark-colored crayon, and an indoor/outdoor thermometer.

Background Information

A forest goes through stages, each supporting its own distinct kinds of trees and wildlife. At first, there may be only low-growing weeds that support mainly insects and mice. As meadow grasses and larger shrubs appear, rabbits, snakes, and ground-nesting birds move in. Then young pines spring up, and the meadow grasses are replaced by plants that grow well in shade. The animals that live in the meadow also leave and are replaced by new plant eaters and predators that prey on them. Soon broadleaf trees, such as oaks, that do well in shade, fill in the openings between the pines, creating a mixed forest. Eventually, as other trees die, the forest becomes almost entirely one type of tree. Such a restricted forest is called a climax forest. Fires often clear the land, restarting the cycle and opening this restricted region up to new varieties of life again.

A tree's most familiar parts are its bark and its leaves. Each different type of tree has a unique kind of leaf and bark. Recognizing differences in these features can be used to identify trees. The bark is actually a protective outer coating not unlike skin. It is composed of an outer layer of dead, corky cells and an inner layer of living tissue cells. This living layer constantly produces more cells, making the tree grow bigger around. Some of the outer, dead layer regularly cracks and peels off and is replaced as some of the inner bark cells die. The leaves are actually the tree's food factory, producing a kind of sugar through a process called photosynthesis. Trees are separated into two main groups based on their leaves—those with broad leaves and those with needle or scaly leaves, which are usually called conifers.

Beneath the ground, out of sight, another important part of the tree, the roots, draws in water from the soil. The roots of a big tree may extend out from four to seven times beyond the crown of branches.

Teaching Strategies

To get things started, show your students a leaf. Then have them find the tree it came from. If there is more than one of the same kind of tree, tell them to find the biggest tree that leaf could belong to. This introduces your students to the fact that different types of trees have unique characteristics.

Next, have your students measure from the trunk out to where they can look up at the tip of the longest branch to find how far out the canopy stretches. Then have them multiply that number by seven and measure on out to see how far the tree's roots extend. Have them circle the tree at this distance, determining if the roots are covered or encountering any obstacles.

Also prepare your students for this activity by showing them how to tell one complete leaf. Many trees have leaves made up of a number of leaflets. Have students find the end of the leaf by looking for a bud. There will be a bud at the base of each complete leaf.

If the number of trees is limited, have students work on these activities in small groups. Allow time for students to share what they discover.

Extenders

1. A Tree for Me: If you're lucky enough to live where trees are plentiful, try this hike. Give each student or student group a tree leaf from a tree on the school grounds. Then send them off to find the tree their leaf came from. Have them collect information about that tree, using the Tree's Company worksheets (pp. 90–91) as a guide.

2. A Hike for Wood: Divide your class into small groups and send each group on a scavenger hunt, searching for as many different items as they can find that are made from trees or tree products. You may want to compile a class list in advance of the kinds of items to be searched for. This list might include apples, nuts, and other tree fruits, paper, coffee, varnish, and things made of wood and rubber. Have students list each item they find and describe where the object is located. Allow time for groups to share their discoveries.

3. Tall Tales: Trees are the tallest living things on earth. To help your students picture just how tall one of these giants is, go outdoors and measure off 364 feet, the height of the giant redwood called the Founder's Tree.

104

Using the Activities ·····················

Answers

Bark Hunters: While answers will vary, these are four attributes that may be included: rough, peeling, dark, cracked; **Tree's Company:** 1–8. Answers will vary; 4. Answer should be seven times the answer provided in No. 3.

Resources

Tree Flowers by Millicent E. Selsam. New York: William Morrow and Company, 1984. *Trees* by Carolyn Boulton. New York: Franklin Watts, 1984. *Forest* by Jake Page and Editors. Alexandria, VA: Time-Life Books (Planet Earth Series), 1983.

That's Attractive!
(p. 92)

Supplies

A copy of the worksheet for each child. To complete this activity, students will need a bar magnet and easy access to a plastic sandwich bag, a rubber shoe sole, a leather belt, a wooden pencil, steel paper clips, a drinking glass, an aluminum soft-drink can, an iron nail, a tree leaf, a stainless-steel spoon, a rubber car tire (a bicycle tire may be substituted), a T-shirt, a metal fork, a newspaper, and a metal doorknob.

Background Information

Matter becomes a magnet whenever its atoms (the tiny building blocks of matter) line up in orderly rows. While a number of different kinds of matter will become at least slightly magnetic, iron and steel form the strongest magnets. In fact, a kind of iron ore, called a lodestone, has interested people since ancient times.

A magnet can be formed by hitting an object hard on only one end, by stroking the object in only one direction with one pole of a magnet, or by passing an electric current through the object in only one direction. Each magnet is surrounded by an invisible force field that will attract—pull toward itself—objects made of a number of different kinds of metal, but especially iron and steel. An electric current has the same magnetic force field around it.

Because of their aligned atomic structure, magnets act as if they have two distinctly different ends, called the north and south poles. In two equally strong magnets, like poles, such as two north poles, will repel each other, and unlike poles, such as a north pole and a south pole, will attract each other. Because the earth acts like a giant magnet, anytime a magnet is suspended in space, its south pole moves to point toward the earth's magnetic north pole. A compass is a tool that takes advantage of the natural north-seeking tendency of magnets to help travelers find a specific direction.

Teaching Strategies

Use the activity sheet to introduce your students to magnets. Have them work on this activity in small groups. Next, present the Invisible Force extender as a demonstration of the magnet's invisible force field and share the background information. Then have students tackle the problem-solving activity described in More Power to You in small groups.

Extenders

1. Invisible Force: Demonstrate to your students that a magnet has an invisible force field. Spread out a sheet of newspaper and lay a strong bar magnet on top of it. Next, cover the magnet with a plain white sheet of typing paper and slowly sprinkle on iron filings. (Borrow these from the high school or purchase them from a supply house that sells science equipment.) The filings will line up along the lines of force, outlining them. For a special challenge, place two magnets—unlike poles facing each other—under the paper and sprinkle on iron filings. Do this secretly. Then ask your students to figure out whether the two magnets have like or unlike poles facing each other. The lines of force curving from one magnet to the other are the clue.

2. More Power to You: An electric current is also surrounded by an invisible magnetic force field. Let students work in small groups to discover this by making electromagnets with six-volt batteries and six feet of thin, insulated copper wire. They'll need to strip the insulation off the ends of the wire with scissors and then attach one end to each of the battery's terminals. Have them try to pick up steel paper clips by holding the wire close to the clips. Then challenge your students to find a way to make the electromagnet stronger. They could wire batteries together, but the simplest solution is to transform the wire into a tight coil by wrapping it around a pencil and then slipping out the pencil.

Tell your students to disconnect one end of the wire anytime their magnet is not is use. Leaving the wire connected uses up the battery's power. Caution them that when attached, the wire also tends to get warm.

Answers

That's Attractive: Will attract 5, 8, 10, 13, and 15.

...Using the Activities ....

Resources

Electricity and Magnetism by Kathryn Whyman. New York: Franklin Watts, 1985.
Experiments with Magnets by Helen J. Challand. Chicago: Children's Press, 1986.
Magnets by Illa Podendorf. Chicago: Children's Press, 1971.

Hot Spots
(p. 93)

Supplies

A copy of the worksheet for each child. To complete the activity, each student group will need an indoor/outdoor thermometer, a watch, and an opportunity to visit each of the locations listed on the chart.

Background Information

Temperature is actually a measure of heat energy or the lack of it. How warm the air temperature is depends on how much of the sun's energy the earth's surface absorbs. Once this energy is absorbed it changes to heat energy, causing the rocks, soil, water, or whatever to heat up. Then the earth's surface radiates heat, warming the air above it. So the air is likely to be warmest closest to the earth's surface. And the air above a surface such as black asphalt, which absorbs a lot of solar energy, is likely to be much warmer than the air above a surface such as white concrete, which reflects much of the solar energy that reaches it.

The form of solar energy that reaches the earth is able to pass easily through clouds. However, heat energy is another form of radiation and is not able to pass through clouds or glass easily.

So the heat energy is trapped, and as additional heat energy builds up, the temperature rises. This phenomenon is called the greenhouse effect because glass also traps heat energy, causing it to be much warmer inside these all-glass buildings than it is outside.

Teaching Strategies

Prepare students for this activity by providing them with practice in reading an indoor/outdoor thermometer. Point out the importance of not holding the bulb end (body heat can affect the thermometer reading). Have students work on this activity in small groups. Provide a class chart for recording the results. Then average the results and draw a class conclusion about the hottest spot, coolest spot, and so forth. Share the background information. The extenders could be done as demonstrations. Fast Action would also make a good center activity.

Extenders

1. Trapped Heat: How much hotter is it inside a closed car than it is outside on a sunny day? Have your students find out by putting one indoor/outdoor thermometer inside on the car's seat and an identical thermometer outdoors on the pavement next to the parked car. Record the starting temperature for both thermometers. Then check again after an hour. The background information explains why this happens.
2. Fast Action: Ask if heat affects how fast molecules move. Vote on a class prediction. Then present this demonstration to test that prediction. Collect two identical, clear, glass quart jars. Fill one with very hot water and the other with ice water. Add six drops of red food coloring to

each. While water molecules are invisible, their movement can be observed by watching the food coloring spread out. The fast-moving hot-water molecules will cause the food coloring to diffuse much faster than the slow-moving ice-water molecules.

Answers

1–6. Answers will vary; 7, 8. While answers will vary, the hottest spot will undoubtedly be outdoors, in the open, in full sun.

Resources

Heat and Energy by Kathryn Whyman. New York: Franklin Watts, 1986.
Hot and Cold by Irving Adler. New York: Harper & Row Junior Books, 1975.
Sun and Light by Neil Ardley. New York: Franklin Watts, 1983.

Set in Concrete
(p. 94)
Soil Search
(pp. 95–96)
Tombstone Geology
(p. 97)

Supplies

A copy of each of the worksheets for each child. To complete Set in Concrete, you'll need ready-to-mix concrete, a disposable metal pan, water, a sturdy paint stick for stirring, and a measuring cup. To perform the Soil Search activity, student groups will need a magnifying glass, three clear plastic cups, three strips each of blue and pink litmus paper, paper tape, measuring spoons, water, and three different soil samples. If possible, allow students to collect their own soil samples. Students will need to be able to visit a cemetery to perform the Tombstone Geology activity.

Using the Activities

Background Information

Concrete is a man-made rock produced by mixing together sand, water, gravel, and gray rock powder called cement. The ancient Romans were among the first known to make use of cement and concrete. They were particularly interested in concrete as a building material because it hardened underwater, which made it ideal for building bridges. In fact, some of the bridges, roads, and buildings that the ancient Romans built using concrete are still standing, and even more amazing, some of them are still in use.

After the fall of the Roman Empire, unfortunately, the knowledge of how to produce cement and concrete was lost. It wasn't until 1756 that John Smeaton, a British engineer, rediscovered how to produce cement and how to use it to make concrete. Today, an improved form of this early cement called Portland cement is used to make more durable concrete. Concrete is also often reinforced with steel rods or pretreated in some way to make it stronger still. Concrete is an excellent building material because it's fireproof, watertight, strong, and comparatively easy to make and cheap to use.

Soil is the earth's food factory. Plants need the minerals soil provides in order to produce food. The soil that forms the upper surface of the earth's crust developed slowly. Scientists estimate that it took from 250 to 1,000 years for just three centimeters of topsoil to build up. Soil forms when rocks are broken down— mainly by water and wind. Then the solid particles mix with humus, rotting fragments of plant and animal matter. Most soils are made up of a mixture of three kinds of solid particles—sand, silt, and clay—although they usually contain more of one kind than another. The best soils are made up of a well-proportioned mix of all three. Sandy soils let water drain away too quickly. Clay soils become sticky when wet and brick-hard when dry.

Teaching Strategies

Have students work on these activities in small groups. Each group could prepare its own concrete outdoors in a garbage-bag-lined box. If they do, have the groups secretly select some items to press into the wet cement. When the cement is dry have each group try to identify these mystery imprint fossils. Explain that real imprint fossils formed much this same way. Have your students be on the lookout for city fossils, imprints of leaves or animal footprints. Have them make rubbings of any they find by laying a piece of paper over the imprint and rubbing on it in one direction only with a dark crayon.

You may want to have students perform Tombstone Geology as a take home activity. Allow time for students to share what they discover.

Either have students work in small groups to examine soil samples outdoors or have them collect samples from home. Then set up a center where groups can test any three of these samples. Allow time for the groups to share what they discover. Draw class conclusions about the soil in your community.

Extenders

1. Rock Hounds: Have your students perform this activity while exploring the school grounds or while on a hike. Have them work in groups to find the roundest rock, the smoothest rock, a speckled rock, a rock that will leave a mark when drawn across a concrete sidewalk, a man-made rock, a light-colored rock, a dark-colored rock, and any others you can think of.

2. Take It Away: What would be missing if there weren't any concrete? Take your students for a walk, encouraging them to observe and name everything that would be missing without concrete. Don't forget building foundations and the mortar that holds bricks together.

Answers

Set in Concrete: 1. It looked like a gray powder; 2. It felt dry and powdery; 3. It looked like gray mud; 4. It felt wet, slippery, thick, and cool; 5. It became harder and lighter in color. It no longer felt slippery; 6. The locations where concrete has been used will vary, but the reasons should include that concrete is strong, is waterproof, and resists crumbling. **Soil Search:** 1 to 4. Answers will vary but should reflect observations. 5. Answer should reflect logical consideration that larger soil particles will allow water to soak in more easily. 6. Should list any soil that was positive for the acid/base test on the chart.

Tombstone Geology: 1. Answers will vary but could include light gray, dark gray, light pink, and red; 2. Answers will vary but should include that polishing made the granite look shiny and feel slick; 3. While answers may vary because of individual conditions, the oldest stone should show the most obvious signs of weathering; 4. Answers will vary.

...Using the Activities

Bonus challenge:

```
E A R T H W O R M  M  O
S O W B U G  V  E     O
O E S O U S  I  P  L
M I L L I P  E  D  E     E
A D U L W I  B  F  G
N M G A B D  C  O  O
T B A D G E  R  X     P
S N A I L  R  D  E  H
C E N T I P  E  D  E
C H I P M U  N  K     R
```

Resources

Digging Deeper: Investigations into Rocks, Shocks, Quakes, and Other Earthy Matters by Sandra Markle. New York: Lothrop, Lee & Shepard, 1987.
Soils by William H. Matthews III. New York: Franklin Watts, 1970.
A Handful of Soil by Seymour Simon. Hawthorn Books, Inc., 1970.

Zoo Safari
(pp. 98–99)

Supplies

A copy of the worksheet for each child. Students will need to visit a zoo to complete this activity.

Background Information

Modern zoos present animals in a setting that resembles their natural environment as closely as possible. So a zoo can be a living classroom, providing an opportunity to study animals in their habitats. One of the most challenging zoo jobs is providing food for animals that eat a varied and sometimes unusual diet. The Cincinnati Zoo, in Cincinnati, Ohio, for example, prepares daily meals for more than 2,000 animals and 200,000 insects. This zoo's grocery list includes huge quantities of fresh fruit and vegetables, liver, meat, and eggs. The zoo also receives shipments of mealworms, rats, and crickets in assorted sizes. Newly hatched "pinhead" crickets are for small eaters like the poison arrow frog. Bigger frogs get bigger crickets. Many of the birds aren't satisfied with anything less than a full-grown meal. But the really big eaters are the elephants. An adult African elephant, for example, eats about one hundred pounds of hay plus twenty-five pounds of grain, fruit, and vegetables every day. Most of the animals also get a vitamin and mineral supplement to help keep them healthy.

Then there are the fussy eaters. The zoo's colony of vampire bats won't drink anything but fresh blood, contributed by a local slaughterhouse. One koala bear on loan from the San Diego Zoo (San Diego, California) even refused to eat anything but eucalyptus leaves shipped in from its favorite California grove.

Teaching Strategies

A visit to the zoo is a must. Prepare students for this by exploring the food chain and habitat activities included in the Little Bit Wild unit. Have students work on the Zoo Safari activity in small groups. If time allows, plan on having the groups also perform the Timely Visit extender activity while at the zoo and arrange for a Behind the Scenes visit. Back in class, allow time for the groups to share what they discover. Share the background information.

Extenders

1. Behind the Scenes: Arrange for a zookeeper or zoo veterinarian to visit, explaining about his or her career. Prepare for this visit by having students write questions they would like to ask. Select about ten questions and have the children conduct this special interview.

2. Timely Visit: Before the zoo visit, have students choose one animal to focus on. Have them prepare for the visit by reading background information in books and encyclopedias about that animal's life-style and habits. Then have them observe their focus animal three different times—shortly after arriving at the zoo, about midway through the visit, and just before leaving. Have each child plan to spend ten to fifteen minutes on each observation, writing down what they see the animal do and describing any sounds it makes.

Answers

1. Answers will vary but could include to pick up things, to blow water or dust on its sensitive skin, to stroke another elephant, to put food in its mouth, to slap at flies; 2. It's an herbivore; 3. This gives the impression of grass and shadows, helping it hide in tall grass; 4. Answers will vary; living in a group helps provide protection against enemies; 5. Answers will vary; it could be endangered because its habitat is being eliminated, it's being overhunted, or a new predator species introduced into its area is threatening it; 6. They help provide a safe place for animals to reproduce; 7. Answers will vary; baby will be smaller and may look different from the adult; 8. Answers will vary; 9. So it can be almost completely submerged and still see and breathe; 10. Answers will vary; it wraps its tail around a branch, using it like another hand to swing or to balance itself; 11. Answers will

vary; 12. Answers will vary.

Sources

Keepers and Creatures at the National Zoo by Peggy Thomson and Paul S. Conklin. New York: Thomas Y. Crowell, 1988.
Zoo Animals by Donald F. Hoffmeister. New York: Western Publishing Company, 1967.
Zoos Without Cages by Judith E. Rinard. Washington, D.C.: National Geographic Society, 1981.

Wild and Woolly Plants
(p. 100)

Supplies

A copy of the worksheet for each child. To complete this activity, students will need to go exploring outdoors.

Background Information

Technically, a weed is any uncultivated, unwanted plant. The unwanted part may be only one person's opinion. A plant that is a pest to a gardener is a delight for someone trying to stop soil erosion. The weeds that some people find pretty produce pollen that causes other people to sneeze. Weeds are hardy and persistent, growing in such unlikely places as sidewalk cracks and otherwise bare lots.

One reason it's so hard to get rid of weeds is that weed seeds spread in a variety of ways. Some weeds produce seeds in pods that burst open, scattering the seeds. Others have seeds attached to silky tufts that act like parachutes, carrying the seeds away in the wind. Some float on streams, and still others have barbs that act like Velcro to help the seeds hitch a ride on an animal's fur coat or someone's clothes. Finally, still others aren't

harmed by strong digestive juices. These weed seeds are eaten by animals and birds, make a trip through their digestive system, and are passed out.

One of the most familiar weeds is the dandelion. This plant has leaves in a rosette that hug the ground, making it difficult to uproot or mow off. The dandelion also has a long taproot to anchor it in the ground. What looks like a flower is really many tiny flowers clustered together. When this flower head develops seeds, it looks like a ball of white fluff. It's really as many as 300 seeds attached to a bit of fluff. To some people, the dandelion isn't a weed, it's delicious. The leaves are eaten in salads, the blossoms are fried, and the roots are cooked like carrots.

Teaching Strategies

On a clear, sunny day, take your students for a walk and make Wild and Woolly Plants a class activity. Set up a center for students to try to grow weed seeds. Have students work together to compile a class weed collection to display on a bulletin board or in a class book.

Extenders

Weed Collection: Have students work in small groups to collect weeds—roots and all. Have them press these plants between layers of newspapers. Then top the stack with bricks. After the plants are flat and dry, have students mount each one on plain white construction paper. Have them use plant identification books to try to name each weed. Some they might find include Queen Anne's lace, sow thistle, pokeweed, dandelion, and burdock.

Answers

1. Answers will vary, but weeds are likely to be found in cracks in a sidewalk, in an otherwise bare field, among trash, and in the midst of a grassy lawn; 2. Answers will vary, but weeds could have flattened leaves or stems that spread out over the sidewalk or be tall and skinny; 3. Answers will vary, but the flower may be less showy than plants people raise for their blooms. The stem and leaves may also be very prickly; 4. They would help prevent the soil from washing or blowing away; 5. Answers will vary but should be very high; to make sure at least a few will land where conditions for sprouting are favorable. Bonus Challenge: Results will vary.

Resources

Exploring Summer by Sandra Markle. New York: Atheneum, 1987.
Weeds by Alexander C. Martin. New York: Western Publishing, 1973.
Weeds and Wild Flowers by Illa Podendorf. Chicago: Children's Press, 1981.

Ants at Work
(p. 101)
Gone Buggy
(p. 102)

Supplies

A copy of each of the worksheets for each child. To complete the Ants at Work activity, students will need to observe ants outdoors.

Background Information

Ants are insects. Like all true insects, their bodies are made up of three parts—head, thorax, and abdomen. They have their

...Using the Activities ....

skeletons, called exoskeletons, on the outside, like a suit of armor. For some insects, growing bigger means molting or crawling out of the old exoskeleton and having a new one harden on the outside of the now larger body. Ants, however, like many insects, completely change, going through an egg, a larval, and a pupal stage before becoming adults. This process is called complete metamorphosis because each stage has its own unique form.

Teaching Strategies

If possible, introduce this activity by setting up an ant farm at a center and allowing students time to observe the ants in action. You can buy an ant farm at a hobby store or dig up an anthill yourself. Dump this first on newspaper while you scoop up enough dirt from the hill and surrounding area to fill a gallon-size glass jar half full. Then pick through the dirt on the newspaper, transferring any ants you find to the jar. Continue to carefully dig into the ants' nest, looking for eggs, larvae, and cocoons. These will look like white dots, small grubs, and grains of puffed rice respectively. If you're lucky enough to find a queen, she'll be bigger and shinier in appearance than the workers. Your colony will be interesting even without a queen, but it won't survive very long. Only the queen lays the eggs that develop into new ants. To keep the ants from climbing out, cover the top with cheesecloth, securing it with a rubber band.

To feed the ants, add a drop of honey, a bit of hard-boiled egg, a tiny piece of fruit, or even a dab of peanut butter twice a week. Remove any leftover food after a day so it won't decay. Supply

water by placing a small piece of damp sponge on top of the soil.

Have your students perform this activity in small groups. While they're investigating, have them perform the extender activity Hot on the Trail. Allow time for students to share what they discover. Share the background information.

Extenders

1. Hot on the Trail: Follow an ant for two minutes, measuring how far it travels during that time and describing what it does along the way.

2. Getting to Know Grasshoppers: Go hunting for grasshoppers. When you catch one, have students examine it, noting the insect's hard exoskeleton. Point out that this is why grasshoppers must molt or shed their skin to grow larger. Have them look for other body parts too: the compound eyes (large eyes), simple eyes (small eyes), three main body parts—head, thorax, and abdomen—wings, and six jointed legs. Then measure how far the grasshopper can leap in one hop. Or hold a hopping race to determine which of several grasshoppers can leap the farthest.

Answers

Ants at Work: 1. Ants have six legs; 2. They help it feel anything close by; 3. Answers will vary but shouldn't be long; 4. It will probably pick up the sugar grain with its toothlike mandibles; 5. Answers will vary; 6. Answers will vary; may go around it or over it; 7. Ants usually follow a scent trail, so they follow each other; 8. This mound helps rainwater drain away rather than run into the ants' home. **Gone Buggy:** Pictures of caterpillar, cocoon, and adult will vary with

species; Bonus Challenge:

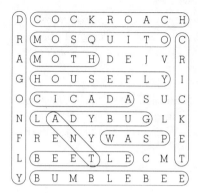

Resources

The Bug Club Book by Gladys Conklin. New York: Holiday House, Inc. 1966.
Insects: A Close-Up Look by Peter Seymour. New York: Macmillan, 1985.
Busy Bugs by Ada and Frank Graham. Dodd, Mead & Company, 1983.

Mission in Space
(p. 103)

Supplies

A copy of the worksheet for each child. To complete this activity, student groups will also need an indoor/outdoor thermometer and a compass.

Background Information

Currently, a United States astronaut's home in space is the Space Shuttle. While this space vehicle is about the length of two tractor-trailer trucks parked end to end, the living quarters are only about the size of the inside of an automobile van. Fortunately, while weightless in space, the astronauts have the use of the entire living area, much as goldfish enjoy the entire inside of an aquarium. Astronauts can function just as well on the ceiling as on the floor. There is no feeling of being upside down.

Every aspect of life aboard the Space Shuttle has to take being weightless into consideration. Velcro strips are everywhere—on walls, on equipment, on clothes—because without being anchored, people and objects simply float away. Bathing is restricted to wiping off, and the toothpaste is a special kind designed to be swallowed. The food is mostly dehydrated to save weight and space. It is rehydrated by injecting water. Water doesn't have to be carried into space because the Shuttle's fuel cells produce water as a by-product. Liquids have to be sucked through a special straw with a clamp on it. Otherwise, once a liquid is started, it keeps on flowing until the container is empty. Liquids that escape become floating balls that have to be chased down and sucked up with a straw. Dishwashing is done with disinfectant-treated wet wipes. The space toilet looks rather like an amusement park ride complete with restraining bars and foot restraints. The main difference is that it has to be flushed before rather than after use because a strong air current must replace gravity to carry away wastes.

Teaching Strategies

Begin by sharing the background information. The extender activity Rocket Launch can also be used as a motivational starter for this simulated space mission. To set up the course your students will explore, first choose an area outdoors. Set a starting point. Next, use a compass and walk a specific number of steps in a specific direction. Where you stop is the spot your students will also stop at in order to complete

End of Leg 1. Now, choose another compass direction and set off again for a specific number of steps to establish Leg 2 of the mission. Keep track of the course you're setting, have your students work in small groups, and give each team a list of the directions to follow in order to complete this course. You may want to schedule each group to perform the same mission at a different time. Or you may want to set up a different exploration route for each team. Allow time for each group to share what they discover in their investigation of this "alien terrain." Discuss together how limited a view of the planet is provided by exploring such a small area. Relate this exploration to man's limited exploration of the moon.

Extenders

Rocket Launch: Have your students work in small groups to investigate what happens to propel a rocket into space by launching balloon rockets. First, you'll need enough monofilament fishing line to stretch a line across the room for each group. Make the line run straight across the room at a level that is easy for your students to reach. Slip a plastic straw on this line before securing the second end. Then provide one balloon for each member of the group. To launch, have one person blow up his or her balloon and hold it against the straw. The straw should be at one end of the line with the sealed end of the balloon aimed toward the opposite end of the line. Have that person pinch the neck of the balloon closed while someone else in the group anchors the balloon to the straw with a piece of paper tape. Then have the person pinching the neck let go. As the air rushes out,

the balloon rocket is propelled in the direction opposite the escaping air. Have each group member measure how far their rocket travels. And have each group compute an average of how far their rockets travel. Allow time for the groups to share their results and discuss what factors made some balloons travel farther than others. (These reasons should include being blown up more and the position of tape on the balloon.)

Answers

1–6. Answers will vary but should be logical for the area students explore.

Resources

Entering Space: An Astronaut's Odyssey by Joseph P. Allen with Russell Martin. New York: Steart, Tabori & Chang, Inc., 1984.
How to Be a Space Scientist in Your Own Home by Seymour Simon. New York: J. B. Lippincott, 1982.
The Nova Space Explorer's Guide: Where to Go and What to See by Richard Maurer. New York: Crown Publishers, 1985.

Sandra Markle grew up exploring science in northern Ohio. Later, she shared the special fun of discovering science with students in the classroom and viewers on television. Mrs. Markle was Ms. Whiz on television for several years. She has also shared her enthusiasm for investigating science through numerous workbooks, books, and articles on science topics. She has served as a consultant to Instructor Magazine and Featherby's Fables, a science series for children sponsored by the Corporation for Public Broadcasting. Mrs. Markle also continues to share her enthusiasm for science through student assemblies and teacher workshops.

Sandra Markle is also the author of Instructor Books' *Hands-On Science*.